I0819606

Holy Momentum

by C. Matthew McMahon

Copyright Information

Holy Momentum, by C. Matthew McMahon, Ph.D., Th.D.
Edited by Therese B. McMahon

© 2026 by Puritan Publications and A Puritan's Mind

Published by Puritan Publications
A Ministry of A Puritan's Mind in Crossville, TN
www.apuritansmind.com
www.puritanpublications.com
www.reformedsynod.com
www.gracechapeltn.com

All rights reserved. No part of this publication may be reproduced, stored in a retrieval system or transmitted in any form by any means, electronic, mechanical, photocopy, recording or otherwise, without the prior permission of the publisher, except as provided by USA copyright law.

First Electronic Edition, 2026
First Modern Print Edition, 2026
Manufactured in the United States of America

eISBN: 978-1-62663-546-3
ISBN: 978-1-62663-547-0

Table of Contents

Introduction

Holy Momentum is not a phrase borrowed from the language of industry, nor from the shallow optimism of the age. It is *not* the power of positive thinking dressed in religious clothes. It is not a man pulling himself forward by his own strength, nor a soul improving its standing by careful discipline. It is something altogether different. It is the movement of a life taken hold of by God, carried forward by His promises, sustained by His grace, and directed toward His eternal purposes. It is motion, but not self-motion. It is progress, but not self-generated progress. It is a life that moves because God moves it.

The Scriptures do not present the Christian life as *static*. There is no such thing as a believer who stands still. From the moment God lays hold of a soul, there is movement. Sometimes it is trembling. Sometimes it is joy. Sometimes it is marked by wrestling, weeping, or wandering through dark providences. But it is movement nonetheless. The believer is always being carried *somewhere*—either pressing forward in faith or being chastened into it. There is no neutral ground. There is no resting place in *self*. The Christian life is a pilgrimage, a crossing, a pressing, a leaning, a longing, and a looking. This is what is meant by Holy Momentum.

It begins, as we will see, where Jacob began—with nothing. "With my staff I passed over this Jordan," he says. That is not merely a historical note. It is a theological declaration. When Jacob crossed that river the first time, he did not carry wealth, nor strength, nor certainty. He carried a *stick* and a *promise*. That is all. The world was behind him, and the future was before him, and neither offered him anything stable to stand on. But God had spoken. And that was enough to move him forward.

Holy Momentum always begins this way. God strips a man of illusions. He empties him of self-confidence. He removes the false securities that once seemed so solid. He takes away the scaffolding of pride, the crutches of worldly assurance, and the comforting lies of self-sufficiency. And then He speaks. And when He speaks, the soul *begins to move*. Not because it has strength—but because it has been given direction.

Jacob did not move because he was bold. He moved because God commanded him to do so. He did not cross the Jordan because he had a plan. He crossed because he had a promise. And so it is with every true believer. The first step of *Holy Momentum* is not strength—it is *surrender*. It is leaving behind what cannot sustain and stepping forward on what cannot fail.

This is why leaning is not weakness—it is wisdom. The world laughs at leaning. It calls it dependence. It mocks it as weakness. But Scripture reveals it as the only sane posture of the soul. "Who is this that cometh up from the wilderness, leaning upon her beloved?" (Song of Solomon 8:5). That is not the picture of defeat—it is the picture of victory. The one who leans is the one who stands. The one who trusts is the one who endures.

Holy Momentum is not a man running ahead of God. It is a man held up *by* God. It is not self-propelled effort, but Christ-sustained motion. The believer leans because he knows he cannot stand alone. He trusts because he knows self-trust is a lie. He moves forward because he knows God is faithful.

And so, Jacob crossed with a staff—but he walked with God. This is the pattern that unfolds throughout the Christian life. The believer begins with nothing but Christ, and finds that *Christ is enough*. What begins as trembling faith becomes steady reliance. What begins as desperation becomes devotion. What begins as fear becomes trust. This is not because the believer grows independent, but because he grows more dependent. The deeper the work of God, the less the soul trusts itself.

Holy Momentum is marked by this growing dependence. It is seen in prayer. When Jacob stood before the threat of Esau, he did not devise a final scheme and trust it. He prayed. "Deliver me, I pray thee." That is the language of Holy Momentum. Not self-reliance, but

God-reliance. Not control, but surrender. The soul moves forward by casting its weight upon God, again and again. Prayer is not an accessory to the Christian life—it is the lifeline of it.

And this prayer is not empty formality. It is not cold repetition, nor proud declaration, nor fearful whispering without faith. It is *living communion.* It is the soul leaning on God's promises and expecting God to act according to His nature. It is faith speaking to God in the language of His own Word.

Holy Momentum is sustained through this kind of prayer. It is also marked by trust in deliverance. "Call upon me in the day of trouble: I will deliver thee, and thou shalt glorify me," (Psalm 50:15). That is not a suggestion—*it is a structure.* Trouble comes. The believer calls. God delivers. God is glorified. This is the *rhythm* of the Christian life. This is the movement of *Holy Momentum.*

Trouble is not an interruption of that movement—it is part of it. The believer does not move forward, in spite of trials, but through them. Trials strip away self-reliance. They expose weakness. They force the soul to look upward rather than inward. They teach the believer that God alone sustains. And so what appears to the world as setback is, in truth, advancement. What looks like loss is gain. What feels like breaking is building.

Holy Momentum often feels like being undone before being built. But it does not end in struggle—it moves toward glory. This is where the doctrine of the Day of the Lord presses in. The Christian life is not merely movement—it is movement *toward something*. There is a direction, a destination, a final day where all motion finds its meaning. The Day of the Lord is not simply an event—it is the culmination of all divine movement in history.

It is the day when everything hidden is revealed. The day when every act, every thought, every word is brought into judgment. The day when Christ appears, not in humility, but in glory. The day when the heavens dissolve and righteousness takes its permanent dwelling.

And this day is certain. It comes "as a thief in the night." Not because it is uncertain, but because it is unexpected. Not because it is vague, but because it is sudden. And so Holy Momentum is not only movement—it is preparation. It is a life lived, in light of that day. "What manner of persons ought ye to be..." (2 Peter 3:11). That question governs everything. The believer moves forward not blindly, but with eternity in view. Every step, every decision, every act is shaped by the knowledge that Christ will return. Holy Momentum is not reckless movement—it is purposeful movement. It is a life lived deliberately under the weight of eternity.

This produces holiness. Not superficial morality, but deep transformation. The believer is not simply trying to improve behavior—he is being conformed to Christ. His affections change. His desires shift. His priorities reorder. He begins to leave the world behind, not because he hates creation, but because he has seen something greater. He begins to love what he cannot see. "Whom having not seen, ye love," (1 Peter 1:8). This is the heart of Holy Momentum.

The believer moves toward an unseen Christ with visible devotion. He loves, trusts, rejoices, and obeys One he has never physically seen. This defies the logic of the world. But faith makes the invisible more vivid than the visible. The unseen Christ becomes more real than the seen world. This is not imagination—it is revelation.

God has made Himself known in His Word. And the Spirit takes that Word and presses it into the soul until Christ becomes the most compelling reality a person knows. This is why the believer can rejoice in suffering, persevere in hardship, and press forward when everything outward seems to resist him. Because he is not moving toward something uncertain—he is moving toward Someone known.

Holy Momentum is fueled by this love. It is not driven by fear alone, nor by duty alone, but by affection. "True religion, in great part, consists in holy affections." The believer does not merely believe truth—he feels it.

It grips him. It shapes him. It moves him. The unseen Christ becomes the object of desire, the center of affection, the end of all striving. And so, the heart is sent out after Him.

This is not passive. It is active pursuit. It is longing, thirsting, seeking, pressing. "As the hart panteth after the water brooks..." (Psalm 42:1). This is not poetic exaggeration—it is spiritual reality. The believer *desires* God. He hungers for righteousness. He thirsts for communion. And God meets that desire with Himself. This produces joy. Not shallow happiness, but "joy unspeakable and full of glory," (1 Peter 1:8). This joy does not depend on circumstances. It flows from Christ. It endures suffering. It persists through loss. It rises even when tears fall. It is the fruit of faith that sees what cannot be seen.

And this joy strengthens the movement. *Holy Momentum* is not driven by despair—it is sustained by joy. The believer moves forward not merely because he must, but because he delights to. Christ becomes not only his Savior, but his treasure. And when Christ is the treasure, the journey is no longer merely endured—it is embraced.

This changes everything. The believer leaves the world behind—not by abandoning responsibilities, but by abandoning ultimate trust in it. Wealth, reputation, comfort, and security lose their hold. They are seen for what they are—temporary, fragile, insufficient. The soul is no longer anchored in them. It is anchored in Christ. And so, the believer walks. Sometimes limping, like Jacob. Sometimes rejoicing, like Peter's readers. Sometimes trembling, like the saints under trial. But always moving. Always being carried forward. Always being shaped, refined, directed, and sustained by God. This is *Holy Momentum.*

It is the life of one who began with a staff and a promise, and found that God was enough. It is the life of one who leans, prays, trusts, loves, and looks. It is the life of one who moves, not by strength, but by grace. It is the life of one who walks toward an unseen Christ with visible faith.

And it ends where all true motion ends—in the presence of God. The staff will be laid down. The wilderness will be behind. Faith will give way to sight. The unseen will be seen. The hoped-for will be possessed. And the One who carried the believer every step of the way will stand before him in glory. That is the end of *Holy Momentum.*

But until that day comes, the call remains the same: Cross the Jordan with a stick. Lean on the Beloved. Trust the promise. Leave the world behind. And move—because God is moving you.

Chapter 1: The Righteous Man and His Seed After Him

"His seed shall be mighty upon earth: the generation of the upright shall be blessed," (Psa. 112:2).

Psalm 112 is a Psalm of wisdom—plain-spoken, richly structured, and grounded in moral consequence. It is paired deliberately with the Psalm that precedes it. Together, Psalms 111 and 112 form a two-handed work: the first exalts God and His works, the second exalts the man who imitates Him. Psalm 111 is theology; Psalm 112 is anthropology. God is gracious, merciful, and righteous (111:4), and now the righteous man must also be gracious, merciful, and righteous (112:4). God gives food to His people (111:5); the righteous man gives freely to the poor (112:9). God's righteousness endures forever (111:3), and the righteous man's does likewise (112:3). Psalm 111 lays the foundation; Psalm 112 builds the house of the godly.

The psalmist begins with a shout: *Hallelujah*—Praise ye the LORD. It is the same word that opened the prior psalm and will open the next. These Psalms stand in a liturgical corridor, each door flung wide with praise. Yet in Psalm 112, the praise shifts its gaze. No longer is it only the LORD's deeds that fill the page; now it is the upright man, the godly man, the covenant-keeping man who is brought into the light. This is a Psalm about what it looks like when God's work takes root in a man and bears fruit—fruit so full that it spills into the next generation. But, in order to understand this, we need to move through the verses in an overview.

Verse 1 – The Commendation of the God-Fearer. "Praise ye the LORD. Blessed is the man that feareth the LORD, that delighteth greatly in his commandments." The man who fears God is the blessed man—the happy man, the well-favored man. He does not keep the commandments as a slave chafing under his master's rod, but delights in them as a son rejoices in his father's wise counsel. The fear of the LORD is no superstitious dread, nor is it the panic of a soul caught in the act. It is the reverent submission of one who knows God's holiness and has set his heart to walk humbly under His Word. Such a man is not only obedient—he delights in obedience. His pleasure runs in the tracks of God's law.

The Hebrew word for "blessed" (אַשְׁרֵי *'ashrê*) is the same used in Psalm 1. The man who is happy, according to Scripture, is not the one who lives by instinct, appetite, or majority of opinion, but the one whose affections are yoked to the Word of God. In Psalm 1 he is a tree planted by the waters; in Psalm 112 he is a tower whose righteousness stretches into the next age.

Verse 2 – The Enduring Legacy. "His seed shall be mighty upon earth: the generation of the upright shall be blessed." This is the verse which holds the burden of my focus. It is not merely the man who is blessed, but his children after him. His seed shall be mighty—not in wealth only, though riches are not excluded (v. 3), nor in fame alone, though his horn shall be exalted (v. 9), but mighty in character, in stability, in God-fearing strength. There is here a generational promise. The upright man does not live unto himself. His piety is not a private ornament, but a public inheritance. His godliness becomes the seedbed of righteousness for his children and grandchildren. His legacy is not in monuments of stone, but in the living testimony of a family shaped by the Word.

The Hebrew word for "mighty" (גִּבּוֹר *gibbôr*) is often used for warriors and men of renown, but here it is applied to the children of the righteous. This is not worldly prowess, but moral strength, godly stature. It is as if the psalmist said: the upright man builds oak trees—his offspring stand tall, and their shadow falls long upon the earth. This is not to imply that salvation runs in the bloodline, for God has *no* grandchildren. But the life of faith, when sincere, is not barren. God is pleased to extend the blessing of the father into the lives of his children.

There is also a corporate implication in the phrase "the generation of the upright shall be blessed."

This is not only about household lineages, but about a people. There is in the psalm a picture of a righteous seed—like that spoken of in Isaiah, "a seed shall serve him; it shall be accounted to the Lord for a generation," (Psalm 22:30). The godly man, by his life and example, strengthens the fabric of the believing community. He contributes to a generation that fears the LORD, a people not swept along by the floodwaters of culture, but anchored in the truth of God.

"His seed" (זַרְעוֹ *zar'ô*), is a common Hebrew idiom denoting not merely immediate children, but one's enduring posterity—sons, daughters, grandchildren, and the extended line of descent. This is covenantal language, echoing the promises made to Abraham (Genesis 17:7), where faithfulness is not severed from legacy. The word "mighty" continues here to carry connotations of valor, strength, and nobility; it is not limited to martial might but encompasses moral and spiritual fortitude. These descendants are not simply numerous—they are substantial, distinguished, and capable. The Hebrew order places the verb "shall be" (יִהְיֶה *yihyeh*) in the future imperfect, signaling an ongoing unfolding of this promise—not just in one son, but in the family line as it bears fruit over time.

The second half of the verse shifts from the singular "his seed" to the collective "generation of the upright" (דוֹר יְשָׁרִים *dôr yeshārîm*). The psalmist in this way universalizes the principle: what begins with one godly man becomes a shared blessing in the covenant community. The word "generation" (דוֹר *dôr*) here is not limited to a span of thirty years but refers to an age, a people marked by their moral character. "Shall be blessed" (יְבֹרָךְ *yĕbōrāḵ*) is in the passive, divine voice—these upright ones are not self-made but divinely favored. There is a judicial tone to the blessing: they are declared blessed by God Himself. The righteous man, then, is not an isolated oak in a field, but the first in a forest planted by the Lord. His faith does not terminate in personal piety; it spills into public good, shaping a generation marked by divine approval.

Verse 3 – Temporal Prosperity and Lasting Righteousness. "Wealth and riches shall be in his house: and his righteousness endureth for ever." Here the psalmist affirms what wisdom literature often repeats: that God, in His ordinary providence, is pleased to bless obedience with temporal good. This is no promise of unchecked prosperity, but a general pattern—one so regular that its exceptions only prove the rule. The house of the righteous is supplied. He is not always rich, but he is not forsaken. He is not always without trouble, but he is never without God.

The emphasis is not on riches alone, but on righteousness that endures. Wealth may perish, but the man's righteousness is remembered. What he builds in faith, mercy, and truth will outlast the empires of men. His kindness is not buried with him. His influence endures because it is not rooted in flesh, but in the *fear* of God.

Verse 4 – Light in Darkness. "Unto the upright there ariseth light in the darkness: he is gracious, and full of compassion, and righteous." Darkness comes. The psalmist does not flinch from this fact. The godly man walks through sorrow, trials, and uncertainty like any other. But light rises for him. The Hebrew implies a dawning light, like sunrise on a storm-worn sea. The upright man may sit in darkness for a night, but he is not abandoned there. God sends him light—not always the light of explanation, but the light of His presence, His help, His quiet assurance. And in that light, the righteous becomes like the One he fears—gracious, compassionate, and just.

Here again, the virtues of Psalm 111 are mirrored. What God is in Himself, the godly man becomes in his conduct. He does not become divine, but he becomes Christlike. And the community around him does not only hear the Gospel from his lips—they see it in his dealings.

Verses 5–6 – Generosity and Stability. "A good man sheweth favour, and lendeth: he will guide his affairs with discretion. Surely he shall not be moved for ever: the righteous shall be in everlasting remembrance." The godly man is generous—not recklessly so, but wisely, guided by the fear of the Lord. He lends, not to manipulate, but to help. He gives, not to be seen, but because he has received. His righteousness is not seasonal. He does not serve when it is popular or safe, but consistently. His integrity is his anchor, and because it is moored in God, he is not shaken. The memory of such a man is a blessing. His life is like the scent of cedarwood—lingering long after the man is gone.

Verses 7–8 – Confidence in Trial. "He shall not be afraid of evil tidings: his heart is fixed, trusting in the LORD. His heart is established, he shall not be afraid, until he see his desire upon his enemies." When the news is bad, the righteous man's heart does not melt. He is not unfeeling, but he is not undone. His heart is "fixed"—that is, anchored, settled, resolved. He trusts in the LORD. This is not stoicism, but faith. The man who fears God has no need to fear men. The one who delights in God's Word does not tremble before man's word.

The psalmist does not deny the presence of enemies or the threat of loss. But he declares that the godly man will, in due time, see the goodness of the Lord and the fall of his foes. His vindication will be public. He may wait long, but he waits with a steady heart.

Verse 9 – Overflowing Righteousness. "He hath dispersed, he hath given to the poor; his righteousness endureth for ever; his horn shall be exalted with honour." Again, the generosity of the righteous man is noted. He does not hoard, he gives. He does not clutch, he disperses. His wealth is not a dam but a river. And what flows from him is righteousness. This righteousness does not rust or rot. It is lasting, because it is shaped by the character of God.

The phrase "his horn shall be exalted," evokes strength and honor. The horn is the symbol of power, lifted high in triumph. The godly man is not a doormat. He may be humble, but he is not weak. His dignity is bestowed by God Himself. He is raised up in the eyes of others, not by grasping for glory, but by walking in righteousness.

Verse 10 – The Collapse of the Wicked. "The wicked shall see it, and be grieved; he shall gnash with his teeth, and melt away: the desire of the wicked shall perish." Here the curtain falls. The wicked, who lived for self, see the triumph of the righteous and cannot bear it. Their gnashing is not only envy, but judgment. They "melt away"—the Hebrew conveys the image of dissolving, disintegrating. Their plans unravel, their strength collapses, their legacy evaporates. What they craved does not come to pass. What they hated—namely, the righteousness of God's people—stands tall when they are gone.

In this way the psalm stands as a mirror. Psalm 112 is not merely a list of ethical instructions; it is the reflection of the man whose heart is tethered to God. He fears the LORD. He loves God's Word. He is generous, just, and firm. He is not shaken by calamity, nor hollowed out by fear. And his legacy? It does not die with him. His children are marked by his convictions.

His generation is better for his presence. He is a blessing in his time, and his name is not easily forgotten.

Psalm 111 told us what God is like. Psalm 112 tells us what godliness looks like in a man. And verse 2 calls men to remember that real piety has generational weight. It is not locked away in private devotions, but sown into children, into churches, into nations. It blesses not only the man but the world around him.

And this—this is where doctrine must begin. Doctrine: *The righteous man leaves behind more than memories—he leaves a lineage that walks with God, carried forward by holy momentum.*

When I say that a righteous man leaves behind "holy momentum," I'm not coining poetry—I'm naming a reality that heaven recognizes, and hell resents. It is the carried-forward force of a life lived in covenant with God—a generational motion rooted in divine holiness and propelled by the Spirit of Christ. It is not passive legacy but active blessing. It is not mere remembrance but spiritual propulsion. It is what happens when grace grips a man, sanctifies him, and sends his righteousness echoing into the lives of others. Psalm 112:2 describes it plainly: "His seed shall be mighty upon earth: the generation of the upright shall be blessed." That blessing does not drift like smoke—it moves like a stormfront, holy and forward-bound.

What makes it holy? The word *holy* belongs to God before it belongs to anyone else. "Who is like unto thee, O LORD, among the gods? Who is like thee, glorious in holiness, fearful in praises, doing wonders?" (Exodus 15:11). God's holiness is not one attribute among many—it is the *perfection* of all His attributes. His justice is a holy justice. His mercy is holy mercy. His love, wrath, wisdom, and power are all holy. Holiness, in God, means He is entirely set apart from sin, entirely above corruption, and entirely devoted to His own glory. He is light, and in him is no darkness at all (1 John 1:5).

When this holy God redeems a sinner, He does not merely scrub his record—*He sets him apart.* The elect are made holy not only by imputation (justification), but by *Reformation* (sanctification). "But ye are a chosen generation, a royal priesthood, an holy nation, a peculiar people," (1 Peter 2:9). That holiness, though imperfect in this life, is real. It is begun in regeneration, fed by the Word, strengthened by affliction, and confirmed by obedience. And it shows. Not only in private devotions or in public virtues, but in children, grandchildren, churches, and nations. Holiness, when true, moves. It ripples outward. It carries weight.

What do I mean by momentum? Momentum is *motion with memory.* It is not a gust but a glide. It is the accumulated force of something already in motion. In physics, momentum is mass multiplied by velocity—an object in motion stays in motion unless something greater brings it to a halt. Spiritually, it could be said this way: grace in motion keeps moving by the Spirit of God, through means of obedience, fueled by the righteousness of Christ by the word. And it doesn't stop with one life. It flows into *generations.*

The righteous man does not live as a lone spark. He is a torch handed down. He walks with God, and his walk leaves tracks. His sons may stray, his daughters may falter, but they stumble in sight of his prayers. His words, his sacrifices, his consistency in the Word—these are not forgotten. Not by God, and often not by men. "The just man walketh in his integrity: his children are blessed after him," (Proverbs 20:7).

To understand momentum *biblically*, the language of *walking* must be used. Scripture is filled with the imagery of movement—especially that of walking in righteousness. "Enoch walked with God: and he was not; for God took him," (Genesis 5:24). "Noah was a just man and perfect in his generations, and Noah walked with God," (Genesis 6:9). "And thou shalt keep the commandments of the LORD thy God, to walk in his ways, and to fear him," (Deuteronomy 8:6).

This walk is a Spirit-led, Christ-centered movement: "This I say then, Walk in the Spirit, and ye shall not fulfil the lust of the flesh," (Galatians 5:16). "As ye have therefore received Christ Jesus the Lord, so walk ye in him," (Colossians 2:6). Walking implies *progression.* It suggests *direction.* And it requires *momentum.* The Christian walk is not a treadmill—it is a forward march.

Holy momentum in the Spirit of Christ is important in this. The righteous man does not walk by sheer will. He walks because the Spirit of Christ dwells in him. The flesh cannot generate holiness any more than a corpse can climb a hill. But "if the Spirit of him that raised up Jesus from the dead dwell in you, he... shall also quicken your mortal bodies," (Romans 8:11). The Spirit leads, teaches, convicts, and empowers. The same Spirit who hovered over the deep now stirs the hearts of men, pushing them onward in sanctified steps.

This walking by the Spirit creates holy patterns—what the reformers and Puritans called "habits of grace."[1] And when those patterns become the norm of a man's life, his influence extends beyond him. His holy momentum carries forward. He becomes a weight in the world—slow to sway, firm in step, steady in faith. This kind of man cannot be faked. He is known in the gates (Psalm 112:8), feared by the wicked (Psalm 112:10), and treasured by God.

And how does Christ relate to this holy momentum? He is the source and the substance of it. The

---

[1] "All the habits of grace are infused into the soul by the Spirit at once." Thomas Brooks, *The Complete Works of Thomas Brooks*, ed. Alexander Balloch Grosart, vol. 3 (Edinburgh; London; Dublin: James Nichol; James Nisbet and Co.; G. Herbert, 1866), 254. And also, "Habits of grace are like the fire of a Smith, be they never so pure and perfect, they burn not in us no longer than they be blown: if God withhold or withdraw his assisting hand, lust draws us aside presently and down we fall." Richard Capel, *Temptations Their Nature, Danger, Cure*, (London: R. Badger, 1633), 10.

righteous man's motion begins at the foot of the cross. There, every backward sin is paid for, every forward step is secured. "I am the way," Christ said, "no man cometh unto the Father, but by me," (John 14:6). Christ does not only point the way—He is the way. And more: He walks with the believer in it. "Lo, I am with you alway, even unto the end of the world," (Matthew 28:20).

So then, holy momentum is not human legacy—it is *gospel* legacy. It is a righteous life rooted in Christ, carried along by the Spirit, and aimed at eternity. It is what happens when a man obeys God over the long haul, under the covenant, and leaves behind not just words or wealth, but witness.

Psalm 112:2: "His seed shall be mighty upon earth: the generation of the upright shall be blessed." This is generational momentum—not mere inheritance, but moral stature and spiritual favor. Deuteronomy 5:29: "O that there were such an heart in them... that it might be well with them, and with their children for ever!" God Himself longs to see righteousness ripple forward. Isaiah 44:3: "I will pour my spirit upon thy seed, and my blessing upon thine offspring." The Spirit does not only fall on one generation—it flows downward by promise. Proverbs 13:22: "A good man leaveth an inheritance to his children's children." The inheritance here is not gold—it is wisdom, example, and covenant grace. Acts 2:39: "For the promise is unto you, and to your children..." The new covenant echoes the old: grace moves generationally. 2 Timothy 1:5: "When I call to remembrance the unfeigned faith that is in thee, which dwelt first in thy grandmother Lois, and thy mother Eunice..." Faith, like blood, can run in families. Matthew 25:34–40: The righteous are rewarded not only for personal piety but for selfless service—fruits of a Spirit-led life, known by their outward motion.

Holy momentum and the doctrine of the blessed generation is to be considered together. God blesses the upright with generational impact, not by natural inheritance, but by covenant grace and obedient living. Holiness is not static; it is *kinetic*. It moves. And when a man is truly godly, he leaves behind more than maxims—he leaves a spiritual gravity. Children raised under such weight often return to it. Churches shaped by such men remain rooted. Communities with such witnesses are preserved longer from rot.

This is why the righteous man delights in God's commandments (Psalm 112:1)—not merely for his own good, but for the sake of his children's children. When he fears the Lord and walks in His ways, he plants oaks of righteousness that may not fully bloom in his own lifetime, but will rise in seasons yet to come.

So then, I say again: the righteous man leaves a lineage, not just a memory—carried forward by holy momentum. The upright man, though often overlooked by the world, is counted blessed in the courts of heaven. Not because of his riches, nor his well-being, nor the ease of his days, but because he walks before the Lord in sincerity. And when God calls a man blessed, there is no higher commendation under the sun. It is no passing compliment—it is a divine declaration, sealed in the blood of the covenant and written in the ledger of eternity. "O the blessednesses of the perfect in the way, who walk in the law of the LORD," (Psalm 119:1). Not one blessing, but blessednesses—wave after wave breaking upon the shores of his life and the lives of his children.

1. The upright are blessed in their posterity. "His seed shall be mighty upon earth: the generation of the upright shall be blessed," (Psalm 112:2). This is not a polite notion, but a thunderous promise. When a man fears the Lord and walks before Him with integrity, that man's children inherit more than a surname. They inherit a trail—a trail of prayers, of example, of warning, and of faith. God marks such a man's house for blessing. The righteous sow in tears and reap in generations. While kings build monuments that crumble, the upright man builds sons and daughters who stand firm. Holy momentum begins here.

2. The upright are blessed in their provisions. "Wealth and riches shall be in his house," (Psalm 112:3). The blessing is not always in coin or cattle, but in sufficiency, peace, and provision from the Lord. The upright man does not scrape to be rich—he walks in contentment, and God furnishes his house as He sees fit.

And when riches do increase, he does not set his heart upon them. He uses them as tools, not trophies. His cupboards may not always overflow, but his household knows the sweetness of the Lord's care.

3. The upright are blessed in righteousness that endures. "And his righteousness endureth for ever," (Psalm 112:3b). Here is a different kind of permanence. The world writes its names in marble; the upright man writes his obedience *into the lives of others*. He may die and be buried in a modest grave, but his righteousness lingers like the fragrance of myrrh. God does not forget the deeds done in secret, nor the labors of love that passed unseen by men. Heaven keeps a longer memory than earth.

4. The upright are blessed in justification. "Blessed is he whose transgression is forgiven, whose sin is covered," (Psalm 32:1). A man may be rich in houses and lands, but if his sin still clings to him, he is a pauper in the eyes of God. But the upright—those who walk not in guile but in truth—are washed. Their sins are covered, not by silence or forgetfulness, but by the righteousness of Christ. The guileless spirit is not the sinless spirit, but the sincere one—the one who walks in the light and confesses his faults. That man is blessed, for the Lord will not impute his iniquity to him. He may have scars from his past, but none of them are counted against him. That is a happiness no man can counterfeit.

5. The upright are blessed in the hope of eternal glory. "Blessed are the pure in heart: for they shall see God," (Matthew 5:8). This is the apex of blessedness—not just to be safe, or happy, or clean—but to see God. The upright are *promised* the *beatific vision*: not a fleeting glimpse, but a face-to-face seeing of God through Christ that leaves the soul forever satisfied. In this world, believers see Christ by faith—as through a glass, darkly—and yet they rejoice with joy unspeakable. But there is coming a day when faith shall give way to sight, and the righteous shall know even as they are known. There is no crown finer, no reward higher. All other blessings flow down from this fountainhead.

6. The upright are God's own people by covenant. The heart of the matter is this: God is not merely generous to the upright—*He* is theirs. He covenanted with Abraham, saying, "I will be a God unto thee, and to thy seed after thee," (Genesis 17:7). And the same covenant stands today. To the upright, God gives Himself. And in return, He requires the whole man. "Walk before me, and be thou perfect," (Genesis 17:1). The upright do not belong to the world—they belong to God. They are His peculiar treasure, His inheritance, His portion upon the earth. To be God's people is the highest glory man can bear, and the greatest duty he must fulfill. A covenant is not a contract of equals, but a bond of grace. God stoops to bind Himself to His people. He promises to shield, to save, to sanctify. But He also

commands: Walk. Be perfect. Be mine. And the upright man answers not with cold assent, but with glad surrender. He knows he is not his own. He is bought with a price—and it is his joy to live like it.

God blesses the upright beyond what the world can measure—through their children, their households, their forgiveness, their endurance, and their everlasting joy in Him—and He calls them, above all, to be His own people. This is not an opinion; this is covenant reality. The man who fears the Lord and walks in His ways will not only be blessed—he will be a blessing, to the end of his days and far beyond them.

Covenantally, God blesses the children of the righteous—in body and soul. God has made a free covenant with believers and their children—a promise not stitched in sentiment, but signed in Scripture. "I will be thy God, and the God of thy seed," (Genesis 17:7). That word was first spoken to Abraham, the father of all who believe, and it still holds fast for every saint who walks in his steps (Acts 2:39; Jeremiah 32:39). It is not an empty handshake, but a sure inheritance, where the Lord pledges to bless the offspring of the upright in every way—temporal and eternal.

1. God blesses them with outward mercies. When a man walks in integrity, he does not just bless the present hour—he blesses the years he will never see. God often sends down honor, peace, and provision on the homes of the righteous. "His seed shall be mighty

upon earth: the generation of the upright shall be blessed," (Psalm 112:2). "The seed of the righteous shall inherit the land," (Psalm 25:13). The wealth may not come in gold, but in favor, stability, and a name unmarred by shame. "A good man leaveth an inheritance to his children's children," (Proverbs 13:22). The Lord, who keeps covenant to a thousand generations, does not forget the children of those who feared His name (Exodus 20:6; Psalm 37:25–26).

2. God blesses them in their souls. There is *more.* God not only feeds their mouths—He feeds their hearts. "I will pour my Spirit upon thy seed, and my blessing upon thine offspring," (Isaiah 44:3). "All thy children shall be taught of the LORD; and great shall be the peace of thy children," (Isaiah 54:13). When God draws a parent to Himself, He sets His hand on the children too. They are received under the shadow of His covenant—"holy," by designation (1 Corinthians 7:14). The child of a righteous father may stray, but he does not stray without prayer behind him. God often takes up sons for the sake of their faithful mothers, and daughters for the sake of their praying fathers. "The just man walketh in his integrity: his children are blessed after him," (Proverbs 20:7). Poor parents may leave no silver, but they leave a better fortune—a stack of prayers rising up to heaven and a covenant promise buried in the child's name. This is why the Holy Spirit presses righteousness on fathers and mothers—not for their own sake only,

but for their children's. "Oh that there were such an heart in them... that it might be well with them, and with their children for ever!" (Deuteronomy 5:29). To be born in a godly house is to be born near the gate of mercy. Thomas Hall said, "Let parents then labour for grace, that they may leave a blessing, and not a curse, to their posterity, Gen. 17:7; Exod. 20:6; Psa. 112:2."[2]

In this, beware a covetous spirit. A man cannot bless his generation if his heart is chained to gold. Christ warned plainly, "Lay not up for yourselves treasures upon earth... for where your treasure is, there will your heart be also," (Matthew 6:19, 21). And again, "Labour not for the meat which perisheth, but for that meat which endureth unto everlasting life," (John 6:27). Riches are not evil in themselves, but they make a poor god. When a man makes wealth his confidence, he denies the God who gives and takes away (Job 31:24–28). Psalm 52 says the man who trusts in riches shall be plucked up and cast out. Riches promise much and vanish quick. "Riches certainly make themselves wings; they fly away as an eagle toward heaven," (Proverbs 23:5). So let a man set not his heart on what he cannot keep.

---

[2] Thomas Hall, "Samaria's Downfal; or a Commentary, by Way of Supplement, on the Five Last Verses of the Thirteenth Chapter of Hosea," in An Exposition of the Prophecy of Hosea, ed. James Sherman (Edinburgh; London: James Nichol; James Nisbet & Co., 1863), 602.

Men ought to seek a heart that trusts God and leans on His promises. "Better is little with the fear of the LORD than great treasure and trouble therewith," (Proverbs 15:16). The man who has God for his portion is rich, even if his purse is thin. "In the fear of the LORD is strong confidence: and his children shall have a place of refuge," (Proverbs 14:26). This is how generations are blessed—not by barns full of wheat, but by hearts full of *faith.*

Christians ought to cultivate a generous, merciful, and public spirit. The man who gives to the poor leaves more behind than silver—he leaves a testimony. "Make to yourselves friends of the mammon of unrighteousness... that they may receive you into everlasting habitations," (Luke 16:9). Giving shapes the soul. It makes the heart warm with love, and the name of the giver long-remembered.

Christian men ought to labor not so much to gather wealth as to use what they have for good. A man may build a fine house and raise high walls, but it is the quiet deeds of mercy that echo through generations. "The generation of the upright shall be blessed," (Psalm 112:2). When Christ returns, it will not be the wealthy who are welcomed, but those who fed the hungry, clothed the naked, and visited the prisoner (Matthew 25:34–36, 40). That is the measure of righteousness in heaven's court. The man who would bless his generation must trade self-interest for covenant faithfulness and open his hand to others as God has opened His to him. All this, godly parents teach their generations.

In the world, memory is often a shallow monument. Men chase remembrance the way children chase shadows—grasping for something that slips through their fingers the moment the light shifts. They carve names into granite, hoping stone will outlast silence. They etch phrases into plaques, mount portraits on walls, or scrawl initials into wet cement, imagining that to be remembered is to endure. But the world forgets its heroes as fast as it crowns them. One war buries the last, one scandal topples a thousand praises. Fame fades, tombstones weather, and the earth eventually covers every name it once shouted.

The righteous man, however, does not live to be remembered—he lives to be faithful. And in so doing, he leaves behind more than memories. He leaves behind people. He leaves a lineage. A holy ripple through time—not chiseled into cold marble, but written on living hearts. "Ye are our epistle written in our hearts, known and read of all men," (2 Corinthians 3:2). His children walk in his ways not because they admire his legacy, but because they've seen his God. His footsteps are not fossilized—they are followed.

Memory alone is a *brittle* thing. But holy momentum is weighty—it's a life moving forward, powered by grace, dragging sons, daughters, students, churches, and even entire generations in its wake. The world remembers in ink and stone. God remembers in flesh and faith. The righteous man's reward is not that his name is known, but that God is known because of him. "The memory of the just is blessed: but the name of the wicked shall rot," (Proverbs 10:7). That is the difference between worldly memory and holy momentum—one fades, the other walks on.

The righteous man leaves behind more than memories—he leaves a lineage that walks with God, carried forward by holy momentum.

And what about your own *Holy Momentum*? Christ Jesus is the source and fulfillment of holy momentum. The doctrine of holy momentum does not hang in the air like a floating notion—it stands on the shoulders of a *Person*. The righteous man leaves a lineage, not just a memory, but only because the Righteous One has gone before him. Christ Jesus is not merely a good example—He is the blazing center from which all true righteousness flows. He is the fountainhead of holy momentum. Without Him, there is no movement, no lineage, no blessing, no Psalm 112. But with Him—by union with Him—a Christian not only walks in holiness, but becomes a holy force in his generation and the next.

Let it be plain. The righteous man of Psalm 112 is, first and foremost, Christ Himself. He alone feared the LORD perfectly, delighted in the commandments entirely, walked in integrity without flaw, gave to the poor without guile, and stood unshaken in the face of evil tidings. Every blessing listed in the Psalm—posterity, provision, perseverance, righteousness, vindication—has its highest fulfillment in Him.

In fact, this is the truth for every psalm in every way good. The "seed mighty upon the earth" begins with His seed. He is the Vine from which every fruitful branch springs. Christ: *The Righteous Man* of Psalm 112! Psalm 112:1 opens with the declaration: "Blessed is the man that feareth the LORD, that delighteth greatly in his commandments." No man, fallen in Adam, has ever delighted greatly in the commandments of God without first being born again. But Christ, born of a virgin, born under the law, came as the only man who ever kept that law with a heart full of perfect joy. "I delight to do thy will, O my God: yea, thy law is within my heart," (Psalm 40:8). He is God, he is God in man incarnate. God delights in his ways and in himself.

Verse 3 says, "Wealth and riches shall be in his house: and his righteousness endureth for ever." What house is richer than the house of Christ? He is heir of all things (Hebrews 1:2). And what righteousness endures forever like His? It is an everlasting righteousness—imputed to His people, clothed on their shoulders, and accepted before the Father (2 Corinthians 5:21).

Verse 9 continues, "He hath dispersed, he hath given to the poor; his righteousness endureth for ever; his horn shall be exalted with honour." Could any words better describe Christ's humility and exaltation? He who was rich became poor for our sakes (2 Corinthians 8:9). He gave, He bled, He rose, and now His horn is exalted—the symbol of His power raised forever.

Christ is the Source of the believer's lineage. Now, if Psalm 112 finds its fountain in Christ, then all its fruits flow into the lives of those united to Him. The Christian is not trying to earn blessedness—he inherits it. As Paul writes, "And if ye be Christ's, then are ye Abraham's seed, and heirs according to the promise," (Galatians 3:29). What Christ earned, He shares. The believer, joined to Christ by faith, walks in His steps, empowered by His Spirit, and becomes the means through which God blesses another generation.

But note this: such blessing begins with being *born again.* There is no holy momentum without new birth. It is not moral reform that carries weight—it is *regeneration.* A man cannot carry others forward in righteousness if he himself is dead in sin. He must be quickened. He must be made alive. "That which is born of the flesh is flesh; and that which is born of the Spirit is spirit... ye must be born again," (John 3:6–7). Only those born from above can set in motion a holy legacy. Only those alive to God can produce living fruit.

And that fruit, in the hands of Christ, is not wasted. "Ye have not chosen me, but I have chosen you, and ordained you, that ye should go and bring forth fruit, and that your fruit should remain," (John 15:16). That word—remain—is the language of momentum. Christ intends His people not to sparkle and vanish, but to endure and abound.

Christ is the Firstborn who has many brethren. One of the most amazing titles Christ bears is this: "the firstborn among many brethren," (Romans 8:29). This is not merely a phrase of chronology but of *pattern*. Christ is the first in a long procession. His life is the blueprint for all His people. He is not only Savior—He is the forerunner, the trailblazer, the initiator of a new kind of family: a holy one. Those who are in Him are called to follow Him—not only to heaven, but into holiness.

And here is where the doctrine of holy momentum finds its force. When a man is in Christ, he is set into motion. The old stony heart is removed. The Spirit indwells. The Word takes root. And that man begins to walk—truly walk—with God. His steps are not only for himself—they leave tracks. His prayers leave marks. His decisions shape others. He begins to operate not just with memory, but with holy momentum. "For we are his workmanship, created in Christ Jesus unto good works, which God hath before ordained that we should walk in them," (Ephesians 2:10). The believer is not spinning his wheels—he is walking in pre-ordained paths. God has prepared those steps. And when he walks in them, the impact is never his alone. Just as Christ's walk changed the course of history, so the Christian's walk—imperfect as it is—can change the course of a family, a church, even a community.

Holy momentum *begins* in Christ. To speak plainly, without Christ, there is no such thing as holy momentum. There may be legacy. There may be influence. There may be reputation. But there is no holiness in it, and no eternal weight behind it. What the world calls "impact," heaven may call chaff. But what begins in Christ never ends in vanity. It presses forward. It bears weight. It carries souls.

Psalm 112 says, "The generation of the upright shall be blessed"—not because of genetic transmission, but because the God of that upright man has promised to bless his seed (Isaiah 44:3). That promise is rooted in Christ, who is the true Seed (Galatians 3:16). In Him, the Christian becomes a blessing. In Him, his righteousness has meaning. In Him, his life becomes not a monument but a motion.

This is what separates holy momentum from *worldly ambition*. The world leaves behind biographies. The Christian, in Christ, leaves behind a *blessing*. These are not the same. The world immortalizes names in stone. The Christian immortalizes faith in the lives of others. Why? Because Christ has not only redeemed him—He has *sent* him. And Christ, being the source of all holy movement, ensures that no righteous step is wasted. "Blessed is the man that feareth the LORD, that delighteth greatly in his commandments... His seed shall be mighty upon earth: the generation of the upright shall be blessed," (Psalm 112:1–2). That man is Christ. And by grace, that man becomes every believer who walks in Him.

Holy momentum starts there—with Christ. And it runs forward through every saint who, having been raised with Him, now walks by faith and sets in motion the kind of blessing that outlives memory and shapes eternity.

Are you cultivating holy momentum in Christ? I'll give you five practices for generational blessing in this. If holy momentum begins with Christ and new birth, it must be carried forward by a Spirit-driven life—one that does not drift with the age, but presses into obedience with resolve. Momentum, by nature, requires movement. The Christian, though justified fully by grace through faith, is not idle. He walks, he works, and he builds—but not in the flesh. "If we live in the Spirit, let us also walk in the Spirit," (Galatians 5:25). The Christian faith does not shy from effort; it only insists that all true effort be the fruit of grace. Therefore, let us consider five practical and covenantal ways the believer, by the Spirit in Christ, may cultivate and pass on holy momentum.

1. Saturate Your Life in the Word of God. "Blessed is the man that feareth the LORD, that delighteth greatly in his commandments." The man who walks in holy momentum is not driven by impulse but

guided by the Word. Scripture is not accessory to his life—it is his compass. He does not read it merely to be informed but to be reformed. "Thy word is a lamp unto my feet, and a light unto my path," (Psalm 119:105). The righteous man does not trust his own heart—he trusts the voice of God, written and preserved for every generation.

Practically, this means daily reading, godly meditation, and application of Scripture. But, not only personally—publicly and familially. In the Christian religion, the head of the household is a federal head to his home. His children must hear the Word from his lips. His wife must see it honored in his life. Where the Word is treasured, momentum begins. Where it is neglected, decline follows.

2. Practice Earnest, Intercessory Prayer—Especially for Your Seed. The man who would leave behind a holy lineage must be a man of prayer. Not just casual, sporadic prayer, but covenantal intercession—pleading with God on behalf of his children, his church, his generation. The Puritans spoke of prayer as the lungs of the soul. A man walking in the Spirit breathes prayer constantly.

David prayed for Solomon, "Give therefore thy servant an understanding heart to judge thy people," (1 Kings 3:9), and that prayer bore fruit. Job "rose up early in the morning" and offered burnt offerings "according to the number of them all," in case his children had sinned (Job 1:5). He did not wait for crisis—he prayed *preemptively.*

Christians who cultivate holy momentum are those who sow prayers like seed. Long before a child returns from wandering, long before a grandchild confesses Christ, the ground has been soaked in intercession. These prayers may outlive the man who offered them—but they do not fall to the ground.

3. Order Your Household Under God's Covenant. Get covenant wrong, and you get everything wrong. Psalm 112:2 makes this plain: "His seed shall be mighty upon earth." God blesses families who are ordered according to His Word. This is not a promise of perfection, but *a pattern of grace.* In biblical Christian theology, the family is a covenant institution—it is the first society under God, and its health often determines the health of the church and nation.

Look at the nation. Look at the Evangelical church. What *trainwrecks.* Follow God's prescription. To order a household under God is to catechize your children—not merely with questions and answers, but with truth pressed into life. It is to discipline with love and consistency. It is to have regular family worship: reading Scripture, singing psalms, and praying together. It is to honor the Sabbath as a family, not just as individuals.

When children see the reality of Christ not only on Sunday, but Monday through Saturday, when they hear the name of God honored at the dinner table and not just in the sanctuary, holy momentum takes root.

4. Maintain Personal Holiness with Public Integrity. The power of a righteous man's influence is never confined to his theology—it is seen in his holiness. He is as holy in private as he is in public. Psalm 112 says, "The righteous shall be in everlasting remembrance," (v. 6). But this is not the remembrance of a doctrinal stance alone—it is the memory of a life that matched the creed. Holy momentum is stunted when there is hypocrisy. Children may learn doctrine, but if they see cowardice, compromise, anger, deceit, or greed hidden behind the curtain, they will not forget it. Paul told Timothy, "Take heed unto thyself, and unto the doctrine," (1 Timothy 4:16). Holiness and doctrine *must* walk hand-in-hand. This means guarding the heart, mortifying sin, fleeing youthful lusts, loving one's wife visibly, confessing sins openly, and repenting quickly. The man who leaves a legacy of holiness is not sinless, but he is sincere. And sincerity, under grace, carries a long way.

5. Engage in Sacrificial Service within the Visible Church. Finally, the man who walks in holy momentum does not keep his light under a bushel. He invests in the bride of Christ—the visible church. He serves the saints, supports the ministry, and models faithful attendance and membership. His children do not hear him disparage the elders, gossip about the flock, or complain about

worship—they see him love the people of God with visible sacrifice.

Hebrews 10:24–25 calls us to provoke one another to love and good works, "not forsaking the assembling of ourselves together." In the Christian view, the ordinary means of grace—preaching, sacraments, and prayer—are not optional. They are the riverbanks along which holy momentum flows.

The man who neglects the church cuts the legs *off* his own legacy. But the man who loves it, plants in it, and labors for it will see fruit that continues. His children learn to value the things of God not merely by catechism, but by affection—by watching their father rejoice in the Lord among the saints.

To cultivate holy momentum is not to be flashy or famous. It is to walk humbly, obey plainly, pray consistently, repent earnestly, and love fiercely. Christ is the fountain. The Spirit is the wind. The Word is the map. The church is the family. And your life—your faithful, unshakable, God-fearing life—is the vessel He will use to shape generations. "The generation of the upright shall be blessed." May we not only believe that promise—but live in such a way that God is pleased to fulfill it through us.

The righteous man leaves behind more than memories—he leaves a lineage that walks with God, carried forward *by holy momentum.*

Chapter 2: Call Upon Me in Trouble

"And call upon me in the day of trouble: I will deliver thee, and thou shalt glorify me," (Psa. 50:15).

If one were to capture the essence of Psalm 50 in a single moment, it would be the dramatic unveiling of the human heart before the Judge of all creation. Here, the psalmist brings the reader to the weightiest of courts, where heaven and earth are summoned as witnesses, and the covenant people of God are called to stand before their Creator. Psalm 50:15 emerges in this scene not merely as a verse among many but as a piercing call to the faithful soul—an invitation to draw near to God in the very moment of greatest need.

The Scene: A Divine Summons. The psalm opens with grandeur and gravity. The mighty God, the LORD, speaks and calls the whole earth to account. From the rising of the sun to its setting, no corner of creation escapes His summons. But as the psalm unfolds, it is not the heathen nations who are chiefly addressed—it is the covenant people of God. Here is a sobering reminder: it is not enough to claim proximity to God without embodying the substance of that relationship. The Lord declares His dissatisfaction with *outward religion* devoid of *inward devotion*. In verses 7–15, He speaks plainly to those who perform rituals but fail to grasp the essence of their covenant with Him.

It is within this context that Psalm 50:15 resounds like a trumpet call, cutting through the superficiality of rote sacrifice to expose the heart of true worship: "Call upon me in the day of trouble: I will deliver thee, and thou shalt glorify me." This verse serves as both a corrective and a comfort, offering a glimpse into the divine heart which does not require empty ritual but for a relationship built on trust, gratitude, and dependence.

Unveiling the Misunderstanding. Psalm 50:15 shows that the reader must understand the misunderstanding it seeks to address. The people of Israel had not failed in their outward religious duties; sacrifices were offered with precision, and the outward forms of worship were maintained. Yet their understanding of God was skewed. They *seemed* to perceive Him as a needy deity, one who required their offerings to sustain Himself or to secure their prosperity. This transactional view of worship reduced their sacrifices to mere tokens of obligation, devoid of the gratitude and trust that should have animated their relationship with the Almighty.

God's rebuke in verses 8–13 is both illuminating and humbling. He reminds His people that He owns every beast of the forest and every bird of the mountains. If He were hungry, He would not need to tell them, for the world and all its fullness are His. This declaration exposes the folly of thinking that the Creator of all things could be enriched by human hands in some way, which is blasphemous. The true essence of their relationship with God was not found in the giving of sacrifices but in the acknowledgment of His sufficiency and their dependence upon Him.

The Essence of True Worship. Psalm 50:15 encapsulates the heart of *true worship* in four weighty movements: the time, the counsel, the promise, and the result. Each phrase unfolds a facet of the relationship God desires with His people, a relationship that is not marked by ritualistic precision but by heartfelt reliance and gratitude.

The Time: "In the day of trouble". Trouble is the great equalizer of humanity because of the fall. It strips away pretenses, revealing the frailty of the human condition and the desperate need for deliverance. In the day of trouble, believers are reminded of the reality of the fall, that ancient catastrophe that brought death into the world and left the human heart plagued with sin and sorrow. Whether the trouble comes in the form of external trials or internal struggles, it drives the faithful to confront their inability to save themselves.

For the people of God, the day of trouble is not an occasion for despair but an opportunity to turn to the One who is both their Creator and their Deliverer. Prayer is the chief part of the thankfulness that God requires in this. It is in the crucible of trouble that prayers become the purest expressions of faith, born out of a recognition of need and directed toward the only One who can meet it.

The Counsel: "Call upon me". Here is a command that carries the weight of divine authority and the tenderness of a father's invitation. To call upon God is to acknowledge His sovereignty, His sufficiency, and His willingness to intervene on behalf of His people. It is an act of worship that transcends words, reaching into the depths of the soul where faith and dependence reside.

The psalmist's counsel to call upon God echoes throughout Scripture. From the cries of the Israelites in Egypt to the prayers of the saints in Revelation, the pattern is clear: God delights in the prayers of His people. Calvin says this command also convicts those who neglect it of impious obstinacy. To refuse to call upon God in the day of trouble is to spurn His gracious invitation and to declare, in effect, that one trusts in oneself more than in Him. (3:20:13)

The Promise: "I will deliver thee". What a glorious promise! The God who commands the faithful to call upon Him also assures them of His deliverance. This deliverance is not merely a temporary reprieve from earthly troubles but a holy act of divine intervention that points to ultimate redemption. It is the deliverance of the Israelites from Egypt, the deliverance of David from his enemies, and, supremely, the deliverance of sinners from the wrath of God through the blood of Christ.

In this promise, the heart of God is revealed as both Provider and Protector. He does not merely demand worship; He invites the faithful into a relationship of trust, where His power and mercy are displayed for their good and His glory. The promise of deliverance sustains the prayers of believers, reminding them that their cries do not fall on deaf ears but reach the throne of grace.

The Result: "Thou shalt glorify me". The final movement of Psalm 50:15 brings the reader to the ultimate purpose of existence: the glory of God. To glorify God is not to add to His majesty but to reflect it, to acknowledge it, and to delight in it. When God delivers His people, their natural response is one of praise and gratitude, a living testimony to His faithfulness and grace.

This response of glorifying God is not confined to the sanctuary or the song but permeates every aspect of life. It is seen in the way believers trust Him in adversity, honor Him in obedience, and proclaim His goodness to others. As the psalmist declares, "Whoso offereth praise glorifieth me," (Psalm 50:23). True worship is a life lived in gratitude and dependence, a life that magnifies the greatness of God.

Doctrine: God's people find refuge, redemption, and purpose in trusting His deliverance and glorifying

Him. This is a key part of holy momentum. The Gospel is readily apparent in Psalm 50:15. At its heart, Psalm 50:15 is a *gospel* verse. It reveals the futility of human efforts to earn God's favor and points to the sufficiency of His grace. The sacrifices that God desires are not the blood of bulls and goats but the sacrifice of praise and a broken spirit. These sacrifices find their ultimate fulfillment in Christ, the Lamb of God who takes away the sin of the world.

Christ's blood, shed on the cross, is the foundation of the believer's confidence in the day of trouble. It is the *assurance* that sins are forgiven, the relationship with God is restored, and ultimate deliverance is secure. To call upon God in the name of Christ is to rest in His finished work, to trust in His promises, and to live in the light of His glory.

Psalm 50:15 stands as both a challenge and a comfort. It challenges the faithful to examine the authenticity of their worship and to move beyond empty rituals to a living relationship with God. It comforts them with the assurance that, in the day of trouble, they have a God who hears, who delivers, and who is glorified in their praise.

Let the people of God heed the divine counsel to call upon Him, not only in moments of distress but in every season of life – let them live in *that* holy momentum. Let them rest in the promise of His deliverance, knowing that He is faithful to His word.

And let them glorify Him with hearts full of gratitude, lives marked by obedience, and voices lifted in praise. For in Him, and in Him alone, do the faithful find their refuge, their redemption, and their reason for worship. God's people find refuge.

Christians ought never to shrink from the small troubles and afflictions that come their way, but rather rejoice in them. These are not marks of God's wrath, nor are they meaningless hardships. They are the very tokens of His goodwill toward them. They should not view them as random misfortunes or cruel accidents, but as deliberate acts of divine permission, designed to refine and strengthen their faith. God disciplines His people not to destroy them but to draw them closer to Himself. He says, "I take no pleasure in the death of the wicked," (Ezekiel 33:11). His purpose in our trials is always redemptive, never destructive.

David gives a key: "And call upon me in the day of trouble: I will deliver thee, and thou shalt glorify me." (Psa. 50:15). God is near to all who truly call upon Him. He withholds neither His favor nor His help from those who trust in Him. When He delivers, it is so we might respond with gratitude and praise. This is all He desires: faith, obedience, and a heart lifted in prayer.

For the faithful, such troubles are *not* meaningless—they produce patience. Patience builds character, and character blossoms into hope, a hope that does not fail. But the world sees trouble differently. They grumble, resist, and blame God, turning to the vain remedies of men. Yet, when those fail, despair consumes them. The believer, however, finds comfort, knowing every trial comes from the hand of a good and loving God.

What is a refuge? In the Scriptures, a refuge is a place of safety—a high tower, a fortified stronghold where the soul finds shelter and defense from every danger. In times of trouble, the people of God have always known where to turn. "Thou art my refuge in the time of trouble," declares the psalmist (Psalm 59:16). This refuge is not merely a physical place but the very presence of God Himself, who is the sure and unwavering defense of His people.

And where is this God? He is not aloof, off in a strange land. The biblical imagery of a refuge draws us to God as the ultimate shelter because He is always near. Consider it, that wherever the Christian is, God is there. The psalmist calls Him "an high place," (Psalm 9:9), a stronghold above the fray, where no enemy can reach. "The LORD also will be a refuge for the oppressed, a refuge in times of trouble," (Psa. 9:9). In His refuge, His people find protection and escape from every spiritual adversary. This is not a man-made fortress but the unshakable security of divine power and mercy.

Consider the cities of refuge established under the law, where those who had accidentally taken life could flee for safety (Deuteronomy 4:41–43; Joshua

20:7). The way to these cities was cleared of obstacles, marked with signs that read, "Refuge, Refuge," ensuring the guilty could run without hindrance. These cities, though temporary and conditional, point to the greater refuge found in Christ. He is the eternal shelter for all who flee to Him, removing every barrier and welcoming all those who are heavy laden to find rest in him, and they come to him with open arms.

To seek refuge in God is to rest in His sovereign protection, a safety that cannot fail. For the faithful, He is a fortress in the storm, a hiding place in the day of trouble (Psalm 32:7). In Him alone, the soul finds its eternal security.

God's people find redemption. *Redemption*, as revealed in Scripture, is the glorious work of Jesus Christ, freeing sinners from both the guilt and power of sin.[3] Old or New Testament is immaterial in the reality of redemption. Both promise the same thing. One is by promises and types, and the other is by performances and the reality of the work completed. It is through Christ alone that forgiveness and sanctification flow, fulfilling the words of the apostle: "In whom we have

---

[3] "What is redemption? It is deliverance from captivity or bondage, or death, by purchase. 1. We were in captivity to Satan. 2. We were in bondage to sin... 3. We were in bondage to the law, subject to its demands, and to its penalty, which is eternal death. Who is the redeemer? The only Redeemer of God's elect is the Lord Jesus Christ." Charles Hodge, *Sermon Outlines: Taken from Princeton Sermons* (Simpsonville, SC: Christian Classics Foundation, 1999), 2.

redemption through his blood, the forgiveness of sins, according to the riches of his grace," (Ephesians 1:7). This redemption is not a partial act, nor is it dependent upon human effort. It is wholly from the mercy of God in Christ, from beginning to end, leaving no room for human boasting.

The scope of Christ's redemption encompasses the entirety of a sinner's salvation. When they call upon God, they get the benefits of Jesus Christ ministered to them. Through His blood, He has "obtained eternal redemption for us," (Hebrews 9:12). This work of grace spans from the first act of forgiveness to the final resurrection of the body, when believers will enter perfect bliss, free from all misery and sin. Ultimate healing is seen in the deliverances of God in temporary difficulties. As Christ Himself declares, "Lift up your heads; for your redemption draweth nigh," (Luke 21:28). This redemption is comprehensive: freedom from sin's penalty (Romans 3:24), its power (Romans 6:6–7), and ultimately its presence at the resurrection (Romans 8:23). Every facet of this salvation is accomplished by Christ, "who of God is made unto us wisdom, and righteousness, and sanctification, and redemption," (1 Corinthians 1:30). The Redeemer's blood, shed once for all his elect, *secures* eternal deliverance for His people. In Christ alone, they find freedom, forgiveness, and the promise of everlasting glory. Let the redeemed rejoice, for their redemption is complete, and their hope is secure.

God's people find purpose in trusting His deliverance. They have a refuge, they have redemption in all its benefits, and now they must find that grand purpose of their life to trust in His time and His deliverances. Trusting God is at the heart of deliverance and the ability to walk forward with him. Trust in God is the steadfast reliance of the heart upon His mercy, promises, and providence.[4] It is the confidence that He will both deliver from evil and bestow good according to His perfect will. The psalmist declares, "Call upon me in the day of trouble: I will deliver thee, and thou shalt glorify me", (Psalm 50:15). This trust is not a vague optimism but a deeply rooted faith in the character of God, who is both sovereign and good.

True trust is fixed on God alone. It is the only thing a Christian can truly know based on the promises God makes in His Word, and the internal testimony of the Spirit to that believer knowing the promises are true, and true for them too. The Scriptures warn against placing confidence in the arm of flesh, in princes, or in riches (Psalm 146:3; 1 Timothy 6:17). Such misplaced

---

[4] "Our confidence or trust in God, and prayer to him, even about the necessaries of this life, is to be renewed daily.
This follows from the words, this day. ...Because there is no day in which we do not stand in need of God's favour and blessing, even in such things." William Ames, *The Substance of Religion*, (CHRISTIANAE CATECHESEOS SCIAGRAPHIA, Latin edition published 1627) 293.

trust leads only to disappointment. Trusting in anything less than God Himself, including one's good works, amounts to idolatry.

Blessed is the man whose trust is in the Lord. As the psalmist testifies, "None of them that trust in him shall be desolate," (Psalm 34:22). To trust in God is to rest in His promises, to hope in His deliverance, and to be strengthened by His unchanging faithfulness. It is the act of rolling one's burdens onto Him, knowing that He is able and willing to bear them (Psalm 22:8).

This trust, grounded in the knowledge of God's character, is both a shield in times of trouble and a song of praise when deliverance comes. Christians are to trust Him, for He is ever faithful to those who call upon His name.

Calling upon the name of the Lord is a sacred duty. What is the calling? *Call upon me?* Is this a phone call, or shout out a window? To call upon the name of the Lord is one of the most important acts of worship, encompassing both prayer and praise. It is not a mere formality but a heartfelt expression of reliance on God, a holy duty that pleases Him deeply. As the psalmist declares in this psalm, "Whoso offereth praise glorifieth me", (Psalm 50:23). Calling upon God signifies the entirety of true worship, for no act of godliness is more pleasing to Him than sincere prayer (Genesis 4:26; Psalm 51:19).

This sacred practice of calling on God originated early in human history. Following the birth of Seth, when the descendants of Cain had corrupted the world with sin, the godly began to gather in assemblies to publicly and solemnly call upon the Lord's name (Genesis 4:26). These gatherings served to preserve the faithful as a distinct people, untainted by the gross corruptions of the world. In these assemblies, the Word of God was proclaimed, prayers were lifted, and the worship of the Lord was exercised, setting them apart as the sons of God (Genesis 6:1).

Calling upon the Lord involves more than private devotion; it is a communal act of faith. Whether in ancient gatherings or in the church today, this calling unites the people of God in their dependence on Him. It is a proclamation of trust in His promises and a declaration of His sovereignty over all. Calling on God always comes back to calling upon His sovereign power. The faithful, in calling upon God, find both their refuge and their purpose. They glorify Him with their prayers and praises, assured that He hears and delivers those who earnestly seek Him (Isaiah 12:4; Psalm 50:15). To call upon His name is to align oneself with His truth, to be gathered into His fold, and to find eternal safety in His presence through Jesus Christ.

God's people glorify Him: glorifying God through calling upon Him. To call upon God is to glorify Him, for in doing so, believers proclaim His infinite worth and reflect back to Him the radiance of His own glory. Psalm 50:15, "Call upon me in the day of trouble: I will deliver thee, and thou shalt glorify me." This act of calling upon God is not only a request for deliverance but a declaration of trust in His sovereign power, His perfect justice, and His boundless mercy. It is the worshipful acknowledgment that all hope and help are found in Him alone.[5]

Glorifying God begins and ends in Christ. Jesus is the radiance of God's glory and the exact imprint of His nature (Hebrews 1:3). By trusting in His finished work—His life, death, resurrection, and ascension—believers glorify the Father, who accomplished redemption through Him. Christ's victory over sin, death, and Satan displays God's justice, truth, and love in their fullness (Psalm 2; Acts 2:36). When believers call upon God in Christ, they align their lives with this eternal reality, reflecting the light of His worth back to Him in praise and thanksgiving.

To glorify God is to ascribe to Him the honor due His name. It is seen in the believer's prayers, their calling upon Him, which magnify His faithfulness; in their obedience, which displays His holiness; and in their gratitude, which reflects His goodness. Whether in private devotion or public worship, glorifying God is the

---

[5] Westminster Shorter Catechism Question 1, "What is the Chief End of Man? Answer: Man's Chief End is to Glorify God, and to Enjoy Him Forever."

act of exalting Him above all else, confessing His supreme worth in every word, deed, and thought.

The Christian glorifies God by trusting Him in trials, believing His promises even when fulfillment seems distant (Romans 4:20). Through deliverance, they render glory to God, acknowledging Him as their refuge and Savior. This is man's highest purpose: to glorify God and enjoy Him forever, with hearts lifted to Christ, who is Himself the brightness of God's glory.

What will God deliver them from? "And call upon me in the day of trouble: I will deliver thee, and thou shalt glorify me." They are to abandon a carnal way of seeking any aspect of salvation and be set on the right path toward true blessedness and spiritual service. God requires that the person whose worship and service He will accept be deeply aware of their own lack of every good thing and their inability to provide for themselves what they lack. God requires the person whose worship and service He will accept to make a conscientious effort to fulfill all lawful vows made to Him—especially the covenant vow to render the obedience of faith to God throughout life. True worshipers commonly renew this vow on various occasions in which covenant renewal is exercised.

Even the most faithful and upright servant of the Lord is not exempt from trouble. This truth stands as both a humbling reality and a divine comfort. Troubles do not come arbitrarily, nor do they signify God's displeasure with His children. Rather, they arrive by His sovereign design, woven into the tapestry of His purposes for His glory, the good of the believer, and the benefit of others. God, in His wisdom, prepares His people for such trials by reminding them of their inevitability: "a day of trouble" is not merely possible but certain.

Did he not readily say it in the Psalm? Did he not know that days of trouble come? Of course, for if he ordained trouble, then there are certain prerequisites to be delivered from it.

Trouble serves a *holy purpose* in the life of the Christian. It stirs within the believer a sense of their own insufficiency and drives them to rely on their covenant relationship with God. In this, trouble becomes a kind of means of grace, prompting the believer to draw near to God in faith, seeking His help and deliverance through prayer. As the Lord Himself declares, "Call upon me in the day of trouble."

For the true believer who rests upon the steadfast and abundant grace of God, there is no trouble from which they will not ultimately be delivered. Whatever form evil may take, the believer has the unfailing promise of God: "I will deliver thee." Moreover, God does not merely deliver; He grants grace to respond in praise. The believer's deliverance becomes a cause for glorifying Him, not only in words but in the entirety of their life. As the psalmist concludes, "And thou shalt glorify me." In this, God's purpose in trouble finds its glorious fulfillment.

"The true believer, who depends on the rich and steadfast grace of God, cannot face any trouble from which they will not ultimately be delivered. Whatever evil arises, they can pray to God and will indeed be delivered: "Call upon me in the day of trouble: I will deliver thee." What more absolute promise can be made to a believing supplicant?"[6]

God's people find refuge, redemption, and purpose in trusting His deliverance and glorifying Him.

Are you trusting His deliverance and glorifying Him? As believers, we are often reminded that our highest calling is to glorify God. Yet, the way this calling is lived out can sometimes feel unclear, especially in the face of trials and uncertainties. Who knows what God will bring this week? What difficulties will spring up? What will throw a seemingly hard wrench into the machine? Psalm 50:15 "Call upon me in the day of trouble: I will deliver thee, and thou shalt glorify me." This verse not only reminds us of God's sovereign ability to deliver but also highlights the way believers are to respond—through trust, prayer, and praise; and this cultivates holy momentum in their life. The doctrine before us is simple yet reformational: God's people find

---

[6] David Dickson, *A Brief Explication of the First Fifty Psalms*, (London: T.M. for Thomas Johnson, 1655), 326–327.

refuge, redemption, and purpose in trusting His deliverance and glorifying Him.

How do believers apply this doctrine to life through the acts of calling upon God, going through Christ, and placing unwavering trust in Him? There is a need for calling upon God. Calling upon God is a *fundamental act of worship* that declares dependence on Him. It is not merely about speaking words but about directing the heart to Him in faith. To call upon God is to acknowledge both need and His sufficiency. As Psalm 50:15 commands, believers are to call upon Him in the day of trouble. Trouble days come. This command assumes two things: that trouble will inevitably come, and that God desires His people to turn to Him in those moments.

One must not rest in self-talk of doom and gloom. Life may appear as an endless burden. The Christian in a moment of despair may begin to think,

> "Woe is me, for I am undone! Everything I touch crumbles, and every effort I make seems to fall short. What good am I, really? I fail in my duties, stumble in my prayers, and fall into the same sins I promised God I'd forsake. Surely, I'm nothing but a disappointment to Him. I can't be like the saints who sang in prison or stood steadfast in the fire. I barely make it through the day without doubting, complaining, or despairing. My faith is so weak—if it's even real at all. I hear sermons

> about joy and peace, but they often feel distant, like treasures locked away from someone as unworthy as I am. And now, trouble has come again. I prayed, and yet here it is, relentless and unyielding trouble. Perhaps God is tired of hearing from me, or perhaps He's decided I'm not worth the effort anymore. I feel so alone, as though my cries echo into a void, unanswered and unheard. Is this what it means to follow Christ? To be constantly reminded of my failure and inadequacy? The promises of God seem like a distant light, flickering faintly, too far to reach. And so I sink lower, wondering if I'll ever truly know the comfort and deliverance I read about but rarely feel."

This is a terrible way of self-talk. It is what can be called *talk of forgetfulness*. This kind of Christian has forgotten everything learned about God. One may ask why Jesus gives the sacraments of remembrance, because emotions often cloud the judgment of otherwise very strong Christians who fall into thoughts like this.

In the face of trouble, the Christian should remember,

> "Blessed am I, for I am redeemed! Though trials press hard and burdens feel heavy, I am not forsaken. God has called me by name; I am His (Isaiah 43:1). My sins, though they were scarlet,

have been washed white as snow through the blood of Christ (Isaiah 1:18). I am not left to my own strength, for the Spirit of God dwells within me, interceding with groanings too deep for words (Romans 8:26). Though I stumble, the Lord upholds me with His hand (Psalm 37:24). My faith may feel small, but even a mustard seed of faith rests upon the infinite strength of Christ. The promises of God are not distant; they are yes and amen in Him (2 Corinthians 1:20). Trouble may come, but it is never purposeless. It is refining me, making me more like my Savior. These light afflictions are but for a moment and are working for me an eternal weight of glory beyond all comparison (2 Corinthians 4:17). I am not defined by my failures but by Christ's righteousness. I am not forgotten; I am engraved on the palms of His hands (Isaiah 49:16). Though the world may falter, my God is the Rock of my salvation, and His steadfast love never fails. He hears my prayers, He is near in my brokenness, and He will deliver me in His perfect time (Psalm 34:17-19). I will rejoice, for I am His, and He is mine."

Trouble is not an interruption in the believer's life but a divinely appointed *means of grace.* Trials expose frailty and strip away illusions of self-sufficiency. In those moments, there is a reminder that no one can sustain themselves, nor find true refuge in the things of this world. How often does one lean on personal understanding or turn to human solutions only to find them insufficient? That kind of self-talk does not help. Calling upon God shifts the focus from self to Him, acknowledging that He alone can deliver, based on the truth.

When believers call upon God, they are not seeking help from a distant or indifferent deity. They are calling upon the covenant-keeping Lord who has invited them to approach Him through Christ. He assures them of His willingness to hear and answer: "Call unto me, and I will answer thee, and shew thee great and mighty things, which thou knowest not," (Jeremiah 33:3). This is not an empty promise but a tender invitation from a loving Father who desires to be glorified in reliance upon Him.

Believers must cultivate the habit of calling upon God daily, not only in crises but in every aspect of life. It must not wait until the day of trouble to exercise this act of faith. Prayer must be the first response, not the last resort. By calling upon Him regularly, dependence and trust deepen, so that when trouble comes, there is already an established pattern of seeking Him.

There is a necessity of going through Christ to the Father in this. To call upon God rightly, it must be done through Jesus Christ. Christ is not only Savior but also Mediator, the one through whom access to the Father is granted. Without Him, none could dare to come before a holy God. As Hebrews reminds, Christ has opened for believers a new and living way by His blood (Hebrews 10:19-20). When calling upon God, it is Christ's merit and righteousness that make prayers acceptable.

The need to go through Christ shows the depth of dependence on Him. Prayers, though often weak and imperfect, are made powerful because they are offered in His name. His name is used on the call, and God hears. Jesus Himself assures, "Whatsoever ye shall ask the Father in my name, he will give it you," (John 16:23). This promise invites approach to God with boldness, not because of human worth, but because of who Christ is.
Moreover, Christ's role as Mediator reminds us that deliverance is rooted in His redemptive work. Every answer to prayer, every act of deliverance, flows from the cross. It is there that Christ triumphed over sin, death, and Satan, securing the right to call upon God and the assurance of His help.

As believers call upon God, they must consciously approach Him through Christ. In prayer, there must be acknowledgment that it is only through His blood and intercession that access to the throne of grace is granted. This deepens humility and strengthens confidence. Believers come not as strangers, but as children of God, adopted through Christ and welcomed into His presence.

Trust, then, is the foundation of calling upon God. Without trust, prayer becomes a mere formality, lacking the faith that pleases Him. To trust God is to rest in His character and promises, even when circumstances seem to contradict them. Psalm 50:15 assures that when He is called upon, He will deliver. This is not a conditional promise but an absolute one. God's faithfulness is the bedrock of confidence.

Trusting God also means recognizing that His deliverance may not always align with human expectations. One may pray for relief from a trial, yet God may use that trial to refine. True trust does not demand immediate answers but rests in the assurance that God's timing and ways are perfect. As Isaiah declares, "Thou wilt keep him in perfect peace, whose mind is stayed on thee: because he trusteth in thee," (Isaiah 26:3).

Such trust glorifies God because it declares His worthiness to be relied upon. When He is trusted, His sovereignty, wisdom, and love are affirmed. This trust, expressed through prayer and patient waiting, is an act of worship. It proclaims that hope is not in human solutions but in the living God.

Trust requires surrender, a willingness to place life in God's hands, knowing that He works all things for good and His glory (Romans 8:28).

What is the outcome to this? Deliverance? Glorifying God? When believers call upon God, go through Christ, and trust in Him, they are assured of deliverance. This deliverance may take many forms: relief from trouble, strength to endure, or ultimate victory in eternity. Whatever the outcome, God's promise stands: "I will deliver thee." This assurance is a source of immense comfort for believers, for it reminds them that no trial is beyond God's power to overcome.

Yet deliverance is not the final goal; *glorifying God is.* When God delivers, He does so not only for the benefit of His people but for His glory. The response to His deliverance must be one of praise and thanksgiving. As Psalm 50:15 concludes, "And thou shalt glorify me." This glorification is the natural overflow of a heart that has experienced God's grace and power.

Glorifying God is not limited to words of praise but extends to a life that reflects His worth. When believers trust Him in trials, they glorify Him by declaring that He is worthy of confidence. When they proclaim His faithfulness to others, they glorify Him by exalting His name. In every act of worship and obedience, they reflect back to God the radiance of His own glory.

Let it be a habit to praise God not only after deliverance but also, in the midst of trials. Gratitude and worship should characterize the response to every act of His grace. Moreover, there must be testimony to His faithfulness, encouraging others to trust Him as well. Lives marked by trust and thanksgiving become a living testimony to the greatness of God.

The doctrine of Psalm 50:15 calls to a life of dependence, trust, and worship. As God's people, there is refuge, redemption, and purpose in calling upon Him, going through Christ, and trusting His deliverance. This is not merely a duty but a privilege—to approach the throne of grace, to rest in His promises, and to glorify Him in all things. In that way, Christians pick up speed – that holy momentum carries them forward in their walk.

In times of trouble, there must be no, turning to self, to self-talk, or to the fleeting securities of this world. Instead, there must be calling upon God with hearts full of faith, trusting that He will deliver according to His perfect will. And when He does, there must be glorifying of Him, not only with lips but with lives that reflect His glory. For this is the purpose of His people: to declare His worth and enjoy Him forever.

Chapter 3: The Day of the Lord

"But the day of the Lord will come as a thief in the night; in the which the heavens shall pass away with a great noise, and the elements shall melt with fervent heat, the earth also and the works that are therein shall be burned up. Seeing then that all these things shall be dissolved, what manner of persons ought ye to be in all holy conversation and godliness, Looking for and hasting unto the coming of the day of God, wherein the heavens being on fire shall be dissolved, and the elements shall melt with fervent heat? Nevertheless we, according to his promise, look for new heavens and a new earth, wherein dwelleth righteousness. Wherefore, beloved, seeing that ye look for such things, be diligent that ye may be found of him in peace, without spot, and blameless," (2 Peter 3:10–14).

The passage in 2 Peter 3:10–14 unfolds with a vivid and sobering description of the Day of the Lord, emphasizing the unexpected nature of Christ's return and the cosmic upheaval that will accompany it. The text invites readers into a meditation on divine judgment and the believer's call to holiness in anticipation of this eschatological event. It is an invitation to be in forward movement towards the finishing of the race, to finish well.

Peter employs the imagery of a thief to show the sudden and unanticipated nature of the Lord's coming: "But the day of the Lord will come as a thief," (3:10). This metaphor, echoed in other scriptural contexts (cf. 1 Thessalonians 5:2), conveys the urgency of spiritual vigilance. The textual variations in early manuscripts, such as the inclusion of "in the night," add depth to the idea of unexpectedness. This is a day that arrives without warning, calling for readiness, as its coming disrupts complacency and mocks human calculations.

Peter paints an apocalyptic vision of the heavens dissolving with a roar and the elements melting with intense heat. The language is both literal and symbolic, reflecting a judgment that transcends human comprehension. Words like "elements" (στοιχεῖα *stoicheia*) invite interpretive debate, ranging from the basic physical components of the cosmos to celestial bodies such as the sun and stars. Regardless of the precise meaning, the text is clear: the very fabric of creation will be subjected to divine purification.

The term εὑρεθήσεται (*heurēthēsetai*) introduces a significant textual variant. Some manuscripts suggest "will be burned up," while others lean toward "will vanish." This "ambiguity" reflects the overwhelming completeness of the judgment, where all human endeavors are exposed, judged, or consumed by divine fire. It challenges readers to consider the fleeting nature of earthly achievements and the enduring significance of righteousness.

In response to the certainty of cosmic dissolution, Peter shifts focus to the ethical implications for believers: "Seeing then that all these things shall be dissolved, what manner of persons ought ye to be in all holy conversation and godliness," (3:11). Holy momentum! The rhetorical question is both an exclamation of astonishment and a call to action. The anticipated destruction of the current world order demands *lives marked by holiness* (ἅγιος *hagios*) and *godliness* (εὐσέβεια *eusebeia*). These virtues are presented as essential prerequisites for participation in the new heavens and the new earth, where righteousness will dwell.

The present tense of participles like "being dissolved" conveys a prophetic certainty, as if the process is already unfolding right now. This immediacy serves to heighten the exhortation, urging readers not to delay their response to God's call.

Amid the judgment, a promise emerges: "We, according to his promise, look for new heavens and a new earth, wherein dwelleth righteousness", (3:13). This hope is deeply rooted in Old Testament prophecy, particularly Isaiah 65:17 and 66:22, where God speaks of creating a renewed cosmos free from corruption and evil. The term "new" (καινός *kainos*) here signifies not merely a chronological replacement but a qualitative reformation, reflecting a reality superior to the present order.

The new creation is described as a realm where righteousness (δικαιοσύνη *dikaiosynē*) permanently resides, contrasting sharply with the transient and sinful nature of the current world. This vision provides a powerful motivation for believers to pursue lives that align with God's will.

To be "found in peace" is a call to a life of readiness, a heart fixed on the eternal horizon where Christ reigns supreme. This phrase carries the weight of spiritual sobriety and the warmth of divine assurance. It compels Peter's audience to examine their lives, not merely in the light of temporal circumstances but under the blazing truth of eternity. For Christians, to live in peace before the Lord means to walk in a state of reconciliation, both with God and with others, knowing that their standing is secured by the blood of Christ in His everlasting covenant. This peace is neither fleeting nor fragile, for it is rooted in the unchanging character of God.

Living, in light of eternity, requires a shift in focus—a deliberate turning away from the distractions of the present age. The world clamors for attention with its fleeting promises of wealth, power, and pleasure, yet Scripture reminds believers that all these things are passing away (1 John 2:17). Those who belong to Christ are called to treasure the things that are unseen, for they are eternal (2 Corinthians 4:18). The faithful anchor their hope in the kingdom that cannot be shaken, where Christ Himself is the cornerstone (Hebrews 12:28).

This eternal perspective transforms *daily living* for Christians. To be found in peace is not a passive state of waiting but an active pursuit of holiness, as Peter exhorts: "Be diligent that ye may be found of Him in peace, without spot, and blameless," (2 Peter 3:14). Diligence involves striving against sin, cultivating hearts of gratitude, and persevering in prayer. Through these means of grace, believers grow in the knowledge of Christ and the assurance of salvation.

Living, in light of eternity involves embracing the reality of Christ's imminent return. The promise of His coming should stir in believers a sense of joyful anticipation and holy reverence. Christians are pilgrims journeying toward a heavenly homeland, where every tear will be wiped away and every wrong will be made right. The knowledge that they will one day stand before the Lord compels them to live each moment with intentionality, seeking to glorify Him in all that they do.

The concept of the "Day of the Lord" carries a weighty duality. It refers both to Christ's first coming in humility and His future return in glory. This dual nature invites reflection on the character of God's redemptive plan, which unfolds in two stages: the inaugurated reign of Christ and its ultimate consummation.

In His first coming, the "Day of the Lord" was marked by grace and salvation. Jesus came as the suffering servant, fulfilling the prophecies of Isaiah, where He was "despised and rejected of men; a man of sorrows, and acquainted with grief," (Isaiah 53:3). This initial day revealed God's immense patience, as Peter highlights in 2 Peter 3:9: "The Lord is not slack concerning His promise, as some men count slackness; but is longsuffering to us-ward, not willing that any should perish, but that all should come to repentance." As if a person would say, we thought there would be more, and sooner.

Christ's incarnation inaugurated the era of salvation, during which the gospel invitation is extended to the ends of the earth (which has already occurred). The mercy of God is displayed in this "day," offering peace and reconciliation through the atoning sacrifice of His Son.

Yet the future "Day of the Lord" is described as a day of judgment and renewal. It will come suddenly, "as a thief in the night," (2 Peter 3:10), bringing with it the final reckoning of all creation. This day will not be characterized by patience but by the fulfillment of divine justice. The heavens will pass away with a great noise, the elements will melt with fervent heat, and the earth and its works will be laid bare. Peter uses vivid language to emphasize the totality and inevitability of this coming event, urging believers to consider its implications for holy living.

The duality of these two "days" shows the comprehensive scope of God's purposes. The first coming of Christ provided the foundation for salvation, making the gospel *the power of God unto salvation* for everyone who believes (Romans 1:16). The second coming will reveal the completion of redemption, where the righteous will enter into eternal life and the unrighteous will face eternal separation from God. Together, these events portray the fullness of God's character: His love and mercy on the one hand, and His justice and holiness on the other.

Peter's exhortation to believers bridges these two aspects of the "Day of the Lord." He calls them to live, in light of both the grace extended in Christ's first coming and the accountability awaiting in His second. The knowledge of the Lord's return prompts an active pursuit of godliness, as Peter writes: "Seeing then that all these things shall be dissolved, what manner of persons ought ye to be in all holy conversation and godliness," (2 Peter 3:11). This dual emphasis—on salvation and judgment—fuels both hope and reverence.

Ultimately, the dual nature of the "Day of the Lord" reminds believers of the faithfulness of God. Just as Christ came the first time, fulfilling every promise of the Scriptures, so He will come again. This certainty compels Christians to live with eternity in view, striving to be found in peace, without spot, and blameless before Him. In this tension between the already and the not yet, the people of God are called to walk by faith (holy momentum), eagerly awaiting the glorious completion of all things.

The eschatological vision in 2 Peter 3:10–14 invites readers to reflect on the fleeting nature of the present world and the enduring reality of God's kingdom. The imagery of a thief in the night, the roaring heavens, and the consuming fire calls for vigilance, humility, and transformation. Believers are not merely spectators but active participants in this cosmic drama, called to live holy and godly lives as they eagerly await the fulfillment of God's promises. In the face of divine judgment, the hope of a new creation shines brightly, offering a future where righteousness reigns and peace is eternal.

Doctrine: The greatest day in the universe is the Day of the Lord. The Old Testament speaks of the "Day of the Lord" as both a terror to the wicked and a hope to the faithful, a day when the Almighty intervenes in history to judge, redeem, and establish His reign. Like a tempest brewing on the horizon, the theme gathers strength from Genesis to the Prophets, shaping one's understanding of divine justice and mercy. In Genesis 3:8, Adam and Eve hide themselves from "the voice of the Lord God walking in the garden in the cool of the day." Far from a tranquil stroll, this verse reveals the first judgment theophany—a precursor to the Day of the Lord. The reformed scholar argues that the "voice" (Hebrew קוֹל *qôl*) signifies the roaring of God's approach, akin to thunder before a storm, as in Exodus 19:16: "And it came to pass on the third day in the morning, that there were thunders and lightnings, and a thick cloud upon the mount, and the voice of the trumpet exceeding loud; so that all the people that was in the camp trembled." The parallel is clear—God's coming shakes creation, whether in Eden or Sinai.

The Pentateuch foreshadows the Day of the Lord further through covenant warnings. Deuteronomy 28:15 declares, "But it shall come to pass, if thou wilt not hearken unto the voice of the Lord thy God, to observe to do all his commandments... all these curses shall come upon thee, and overtake thee." The covenant curses echo through the prophets, particularly in Joel and Zephaniah, as they describe divine judgment that will sweep over nations like a consuming fire.

Consider Joel's chilling words in Joel 2:1–2: "Blow ye the trumpet in Zion, and sound an alarm in my holy mountain: let all the inhabitants of the land tremble: for the day of the Lord cometh, for it is nigh at hand; a day of darkness and of gloominess, a day of clouds and of thick darkness." The imagery hearkens back to the darkness of Sinai and the plagues of Egypt, where God's judgment disrupted the natural order. In Exodus 10:22, Moses stretched out his hand, and "there was a thick darkness in all the land of Egypt three days." Such scenes foreshadow the eschatological Day of the Lord, a climactic intervention of God into human history.

The Day of the Lord also reveals God's mercy amidst judgment. Isaiah proclaims, "Come, my people, enter thou into thy chambers, and shut thy doors about thee: hide thyself as it were for a little moment, until the indignation be overpast," (Isaiah 26:20). For the faithful remnant, the Day holds the promise of deliverance. As Zephaniah declares in Zephaniah 3:17, "The Lord thy God in the midst of thee is mighty; he will save, he will rejoice over thee with joy; he will rest in his love, he will joy over thee with singing."

Yet this hope does not negate the certainty of judgment. Amos warns in Amos 5:18, "Woe unto you that desire the day of the Lord! To what end is it for you? The day of the Lord is darkness, and not light." The dual nature of the Day ensures it brings condemnation for the rebellious and vindication for the faithful.

This duality is consistent throughout the Old Testament. The golden calf incident in Exodus 32 exemplifies God's justice and mercy *intertwined*. Though He spares Israel from annihilation, He does not leave sin unpunished, declaring, "In the day when I visit I will visit their sin upon them," (Exodus 32:34). Likewise, Isaiah's prophecies of destruction are interwoven with visions of restoration: "And it shall come to pass in the last days, that the mountain of the Lord's house shall be established... and all nations shall flow unto it," (Isaiah 2:2).

The prophets understood the Day of the Lord as both a present reality and an ultimate culmination. Past events of judgment—such as the flood in Genesis 7:23, where "every living substance was destroyed which was upon the face of the ground"—serve as patterns for the final Day when God will judge all nations. Malachi encapsulates this duality: "For, behold, the day cometh, that shall burn as an oven; and all the proud... shall be stubble... But unto you that fear my name shall the Sun of righteousness arise with healing in his wings," (Malachi 4:1–2).

The Day of the Lord in the Old Testament is in this way a blazing fire and a warm light. It warns of God's justice, unflinching and inescapable, yet promises redemption for those who trust in Him. It is a day that speaks to every generation, urging repentance while pointing to the future reign of the righteous King. As the Psalmist declares, "The Lord shall judge the people with equity... for he cometh to judge the earth: he shall judge the world with righteousness, and the people with his truth," (Psalm 96:10,13). Such is the Day of the Lord: a consuming fire to the wicked and an eternal refuge for the redeemed.

The Day of the Lord in its dual nature is important. The Day of the Lord, or the Day of Christ refers first to the time of Christ's earthly ministry: when Christ came to live among humanity as the God-Man to fulfill the covenant of redemption. As mentioned in Luke 17:22, "Ye shall desire to see one of the days of the Son of man." This period is also described as "the days of his flesh" in Hebrews 5:7: "In the days of his flesh, when he had offered up prayers and supplications with strong crying and tears..." Additionally, Malachi 4:1 speaks to this time. "For, behold, the day cometh, that shall burn as an oven;" (Mal. 4:1). Even the Christian Sabbath, referred to as the "Lord's Day" in Revelation 1:10: "I was in the Spirit on the Lord's Day," also points to this, a marker of what Christ came to do.

Times of specific judgment by God: The Day of the Lord can also signify moments when God brings judgment upon a particular people or place, as seen in Joel 2:1, Amos 1, and Obadiah 15.

It is fulfilled, initiated at the time of Christ's grace offered to sinners. This encompasses the period when Christ extends grace and salvation to humanity, as referenced again in Luke 17:22. "The days will come, when ye shall desire to see one of the days of the Son of man," (Luke 17:22).

Christ's second coming in glory and judgment: This is the time when Christ will return in majesty to judge the world. Luke 17:24 states, "For as the lightning, that lighteneth out of the one part under heaven, shineth unto the other part under heaven; so shall also the Son of man be in his day." Similarly, 2 Peter 3:10 declares, "But the day of the Lord will come as a thief in the night."

It is a day of wrath and condemnation for the wicked. As described in Romans 2:5 and 2 Peter 3:7, it is a day when the ungodly face destruction. But it is a day of redemption for the godly. For believers, it is a day of liberation, as seen in Luke 21:28: "And when these things begin to come to pass, then look up, and lift up your heads; for your redemption draweth nigh."

And, it is a day of revelation for all creation. Both men and angels will be fully revealed for who they are and for their deeds, as foretold in 2 Peter 2:9. "The Lord knoweth how to deliver the godly out of temptations, and to reserve the unjust unto the day of judgment to be punished," (2 Peter 2:9).

On the final Day of the Lord, a Day of Judgment, every person will be tried and judged, receiving their eternal state, whether of life or damnation. It is the Last Day and Great Day of the Lord. It is the final, climactic day of history, described as a day full of glory for Christ, joy for the righteous, and sorrow for the wicked. As John 6:39 states, "And this is the Father's will which hath sent me, that of all which he hath given me I should lose nothing, but should raise it up again at the last day." Likewise, 2 Peter 3:11 points to this day as a time of cosmic and moral transformation: "Seeing then that all these things shall be dissolved, what manner of persons ought ye to be in all holy conversation and godliness."

After this day, there will no longer be a succession of days and nights. For the righteous, it will be one unending day of light and joy. For the wicked, it will be one eternal night of darkness and despair. This eternal divide reflects the ultimate culmination of God's justice and mercy.

It is the final greatest day at the end which sets itself squarely on the precursor to the greatest day when Christ came into the world to save sinners.

The Day of the Lord is the greatest day ever! The day of the Lord stands as a *monumental truth* in the Christian faith, one both dreadful and glorious. It is a day that will reveal God's justice, vindicate His saints, and display the full majesty of Christ. Few doctrines capture the grandeur of God's purposes like the final judgment, where all of human history culminates in a moment of divine reckoning. This event, spoken of throughout Scripture, offers a sobering warning to the wicked and a joyful hope to the righteous.

It is a stretched day, a then, a now and a not yet. It began in promise, was then in Christ's incarnation, a now for God's combat in gathering his elect to his church, and a not yet to come. "The end of God's appointing this day, is for the manifestation of the glory of his mercy in the eternal salvation of the elect; and of his justice in the damnation of the reprobate, who are wicked and disobedient."[7]

The Scriptures teach that Christ's coming occurs in three forms: to humanity in His incarnation (promised and performance), then within his people in His presence through the Spirit, and against humanity in His role as Judge at the last and glorious day. The first of these, Christ's incarnation, fulfilled the promises of old. "He came unto his own, and his own received him not," (John 1:11). The second continues in His spiritual presence among believers, as He declared, "Lo, I am with you alway, even unto the end of the world," (Matthew 28:20). But it is the third coming, against humanity, that carries the greatest weight in Scripture's warnings and promises: "Behold, he cometh with clouds; and every eye shall see him," (Revelation 1:7).

The certainty of the Last Judgment is without dispute. The day of the Lord is not a mere theological concept; it is a *certainty* established in the Word of God. Christ's first coming in humility was foretold by the prophets, and His second coming in majesty is assured by the same authority. This event, described as "that day" or "the day of the Lord," will come with suddenness and finality. "The day of the Lord will come as a thief in the night," (2 Peter 3:10). No one knows the exact hour, for it is hidden in the counsel of God: "But of that day

---

[7] 1647 Westminster Confession of Faith, 33:2.

and hour knoweth no man, no, not the angels of heaven, but my Father only," (Matthew 24:36).

The Scriptures are replete with references to this day. It is the culmination of human history, where all will be laid bare before the Creator. "For God shall bring every work into judgment, with every secret thing, whether it be good, or whether it be evil," (Ecclesiastes 12:14).

This truth was proclaimed by Enoch before the flood: "Behold, the Lord cometh with ten thousands of his saints, to execute judgment upon all," (Jude 14–15). Christ Himself spoke often of this day, describing it as a time when the righteous and wicked will be separated, like wheat from tares. "The Son of man shall send forth his angels, and they shall gather out of his kingdom all things that offend, and them which do iniquity," (Matthew 13:41). He called it a day of regeneration, where all things are made new (Matthew 19:28). The apostle Paul echoed this theme, referring to it as the day when the secrets of men will be judged (Romans 2:16).

Jesus Christ, the second Person of the Trinity, will be the Judge on that day. This honor belongs to Him as the One who was humbled in His first coming and now exalted in His second. "For the Father judgeth no man, but hath committed all judgment unto the Son," (John 5:22). Christ's role as Judge is both a display of His authority and a vindication of His humiliation. "Wherefore God also hath highly exalted him, and given him a name which is above every name," (Philippians 2:9).

The judgment will be universal, encompassing all rational creatures—angels and men alike. "Do ye not know that the saints shall judge the world? ... Know ye not that we shall judge angels?" (1 Corinthians 6:2–3). All humanity, both the living and the dead, will appear before the judgment seat of Christ: "For we must all appear before the judgment seat of Christ; that every one may receive the things done in his body, according to that he hath done, whether it be good or bad," (2 Corinthians 5:10).

For the righteous, this will be a day of *vindication* and *reward*. Every faithful deed, prayer, and act of service will be acknowledged and celebrated. "Well done, thou good and faithful servant: thou hast been faithful over a few things, I will make thee ruler over many things: enter thou into the joy of thy lord," (Matthew 25:21). Their sins, covered by the blood of the everlasting covenant of Christ, will not be brought forward to condemnation but to demonstrate the greatness of God's mercy.

For the wicked, however, this day will be one of terror. Every sinful deed, thought, and word will be exposed and punished. "Depart from me, ye cursed, into everlasting fire, prepared for the devil and his angels," (Matthew 25:41). Their own consciences will bear witness against them, for even in this life, conscience speaks: "Their conscience also bearing witness, and their thoughts the mean while accusing or else excusing one another," (Romans 2:15).

The nature of this judgment is glorious. The final judgment will reveal the perfect justice of God. Two books will be opened: the book of conscience and the book of God's omniscience. The first records every thought and action of humanity; the second contains the infallible knowledge of God. "And the dead were judged out of those things which were written in the books, according to their works," (Revelation 20:12).

This judgment will not be a hurried event. Every sin will be examined, and every act of faith rewarded. Edward Leigh, "The judgment will not be instantaneous but will take sufficient time to reveal God's justice, vindicate the righteous, and condemn the wicked."[8] The process will demonstrate the righteousness of God, the justice of Christ, and the wickedness of sin. The day will reveal not only individual guilt but also the degrees of sin and righteousness. "For God shall bring every work into judgment, with every secret thing," (Ecclesiastes 12:14).

The saints will stand as witnesses to Christ's righteousness, sharing in His glory as His redeemed people. "Know ye not that we shall judge angels?" (1 Corinthians 6:3). Their faithfulness will be

---

[8] Edward Leigh, *A Systeme or Body of Divinity Consisting of Ten Books* (London: A.M. for William Lee, 1654), 864.

acknowledged before all, and their union with Christ will be fully realized. "Then shall the righteous shine forth as the sun in the kingdom of their Father," (Matthew 13:43).

This greatest day in the universe is a day of glory and terror. The day of the Lord will be both glorious and dreadful. For the saints, it will be a day of rejoicing, likened to the arrival of a bridegroom or the crowning of a king. "And when these things begin to come to pass, then look up, and lift up your heads; for your redemption draweth nigh," (Luke 21:28). It will be a day of refreshing, where the sorrows of this life give way to eternal joy. "God shall wipe away all tears from their eyes," (Revelation 21:4).

For the wicked, it will be a day of *terror*. Christ will come with the armies of heaven, attended by angels and clothed in majesty. "The Son of man shall come in the glory of his Father with his angels; and then he shall reward every man according to his works," (Matthew 16:27). The suddenness of His coming will amplify their fear, as He descends like a thief in the night or a snare upon the unwary (Luke 21:35).

The day will mark the end of all earthly things. The heavens and the earth will pass away, making room for the new creation. "Nevertheless we, according to his promise, look for new heavens and a new earth, wherein dwelleth righteousness," (2 Peter 3:13). After the judgment, the righteous will enter eternal life, while the wicked are cast into eternal punishment. "And these shall go away into everlasting punishment: but the righteous into life eternal," (Matthew 25:46).

It is the greatest day ever. The day of the Lord is the *ultimate* demonstration of God's glory. It brings to fulfillment His purposes in creation and redemption, showing the harmony of His justice, mercy, and power. For the saints, it is a day of triumph, where their faith is vindicated, and they are welcomed into eternal joy. For the wicked, it is a day of dread, where their rebellion meets its just reward. "Those men are without any real interest in God as their God, those that live in the world without making the day of the Lord to be their delight."[9] This day is not merely a conclusion to history but the beginning of eternity (forever always beginning). It will end the struggles and sorrows of this fallen world and usher in a new creation where righteousness dwells. For the believer, this truth should inspire hope and holiness. How shall it inspire the Christian? "Seeing then that all these things shall be dissolved, what manner of persons ought ye to be in all holy conversation and godliness," (2 Peter 3:11).

Living in light of the greatest day ever is a call to walk well, in *holy momentum*. The Lord's first coming was with gentleness, but His second coming will be with judgment and will be unexpected, Peter compares it to a

---

[9] Christopher Love, *The Natural Man's Case Stated*, (Crossville, TN: Puritan Publications, 2025) 224.

thief. Peter, in a stroke of vivid metaphor, likens this great event to the coming of a thief in the night, a comparison that demands reflection.

A thief comes with a design to catch the unsuspecting off guard and claim his prize. In much the same way, Christ's return will seize upon those who slumber in the false security of sin. These are the careless professors who live as though there were no God to revere, no Christ to anticipate, no heaven to gain, and no hell to fear. To these, He will come suddenly, and they shall find themselves taken as prey, assigned to the dreadful company of unbelievers and reprobates (Luke 12:46).

A thief arrives armed for his work, equipped with tools to achieve his aims. So too will Christ descend, not in meekness, but prepared for judgment, with fire and sword. Isaiah foretold it, saying, "For by fire and by his sword will the Lord plead with all flesh: and the slain of the Lord shall be many," (Isaiah 66:16). His angels will accompany Him in flaming fire, taking vengeance on those who know not God (2 Thessalonians 1:7–8).

The thief strikes at a time of quiet, when none expect him. In like manner, Christ will return when the world is engrossed in its daily pursuits—eating, drinking, marrying, and making merry—heedless of the heavens above them. As it was in the days of Noah, so shall it be at the coming of the Son of Man (Matthew

24:37–39). Suddenly, the skies will be torn asunder, the archangel will cry aloud, and Christ will appear in all His glory.

A thief's arrival brings terror to those caught unprepared. The household, surprised by a thief, is thrown into chaos and confusion. And what is this compared to the terror that shall grip the ungodly when Christ returns? They will cry out to the mountains and rocks, "Fall on us, and hide us from the face of him that sitteth on the throne, and from the wrath of the Lamb: for the great day of his wrath is come; and who shall be able to stand?" (Revelation 6:16–17).

The thief's intrusion robs his victims of all sense of pleasure and security. So too, when the day of the Lord arrives, the ungodly will find no comfort in their former pleasures or treasures. All their delights will seem as shadows, and they would rather be extinguished than face the eternal burnings that await. But there will be no escape, no end to their misery, for "their worm dieth not, and the fire is not quenched," (Mark 9:44).

A thief often leaves ruin in his wake. Likewise, Christ's return will bring utter devastation to the wicked. Stripped of their idols, they will lament their folly, crying out for grace too late. Like the foolish virgins who found the door shut, they will plead for entrance but will hear instead, "I know you not," (Matthew 25:12).

But the comparison falters in certain respects, for Christ's coming far surpasses the thief's. The thief comes with wicked intent, but Christ's purpose is holy. Christ comes not for selfish gain but to fulfill His Father's will—to deliver His people from every sorrow and render justice to His enemies. His intent is righteous, His cause glorious.

The thief's arrival may be thwarted, but Christ's cannot. The day of the Lord is fixed by divine decree. No vigilance or preparation can forestall its coming. "But the day of the Lord will come as a thief in the night," (2 Peter 3:10). It is inevitable.

The thief's damage is limited, but Christ's judgment is *universal*. The thief plunders a single household, or a house or two, but Christ's return will affect all creation. "Behold, the Lord cometh with ten thousands of his saints, to execute judgment upon all," (Jude 14–15). Delaune says rightly, "that this truth demands three solemn responses: reproof, caution, and exhortation."[10] Reproof: Let this doctrine rebuke the ungodly, who live as though the warnings of Scripture were idle tales. The Word of God declares plainly that Christ will return, yet they slumber on, their hearts hardened, their consciences seared. Willful ignorance of so great a truth will not excuse them on that great day.

---

[10] Thomas De Laune, *Tropologia*, (London: John Richardson and John Darby for Enoch Prosser, 1681), 280.

Caution: To believers, this is a call to vigilance. Christ Himself urged, "Watch ye therefore, and pray always, that ye may be accounted worthy to escape all these things that shall come to pass, and to stand before the Son of man," (Luke 21:36). Let no believer be found slumbering in spiritual apathy when the day of the Lord arrives. Exhortation: Let all prepare for that day. Only those ready will enter the marriage supper of the Lamb. "Be ye therefore ready also: for the Son of man cometh at an hour when ye think not," (Luke 12:40). There will be no second opportunity after the door is shut. Now is the time for repentance and faith. Now is the time to seek Christ while He may be found.

Though the day of the Lord is a terror to the wicked, it is the crown of hope for the righteous. It is the day when Christ will gather His own, vindicate His name, and set all things right. For the believer, it is the consummation of redemption, the hour of joy, and the entrance into eternal glory. Let Christians hold fast to this promise, watching and waiting for the day when the Lord of glory shall descend. Even so, come, Lord Jesus (Revelation 22:20).

As the greatest day ever, the day of the Lord calls Christians to live with an eternal perspective in holy momentum toward righteousness. It reminds them that their lives are not their own and that every thought, word, and deed has eternal significance. For those in Christ, it is a day to anticipate with joy, knowing that it marks the beginning of an unending fellowship with God. For those outside of Christ, it is a day to fear and a call to repentance. Christians must lift their eyes to the heavens, living each day, in light of this great reality. For the day of the Lord will surely come, and in that day, Christ's glory will shine brighter than the sun, and His righteousness will fill the earth as the waters cover the sea. May all God's people be found ready, standing firm in faith, and rejoicing in the hope of that greatest day ever. For, the greatest day in the universe is the Day of the Lord.

Comfort in Christ's coming is a balm for believers. As much as the doctrine of Christ's return strikes terror in the hearts of the ungodly, it is ordained by God as a wellspring of consolation for His people. This glorious truth is meant to steady us as we walk through this fleeting life, pressing toward the eternal joys of heaven. The apostle Paul declared this comfort plainly in 1 Thessalonians 4:16–18: "For the Lord himself shall descend from heaven with a shout, with the voice of the archangel, and with the trump of God: and the dead in Christ shall rise first: Then we which are alive and remain shall be caught up together with them in the clouds, to meet the Lord in the air: and so shall we ever be with the Lord. Wherefore comfort one another with these words." Peter equally says this but in a different manner. Christians are comforted by Christ's return and they show this by the way they live. You'll know them by the way they live.

Let us, then, draw near to this doctrine with hearts prepared to drink deeply of its encouragement, for it offers consolation in every trial we face. Whether we labor for Christ, suffer for His name, or endure the unjust judgments of a fallen world, the coming of our Savior assures us that all will be set right.

How is it that Christians can heap burning coals on the heads of others that are abusive but by knowing that in the end, all will be made right. Meekness leads to justice.

There is great comfort for laborers in the Gospel in this. First, Christ's return offers wonderful comfort to those who labor in the ministry of the Word. Every faithful preacher, every tireless minister, can look to this day as one of immense joy. Paul himself found his hope and crown of rejoicing in the souls God had brought to Himself through his ministry. He declared in 1 Thessalonians 2:19, "For what is our hope, or joy, or crown of rejoicing? Are not even ye in the presence of our Lord Jesus Christ at his coming?" What joy it will be to stand before Christ and say with Isaiah, "Behold, I and the children whom the Lord hath given me," (Isaiah 8:18). On that day, no labor for the kingdom will go unrecognized. Every soul shepherded into the fold, every prayer uttered for the lost, every tear shed in intercession will be remembered. This is a glorious day of rejoicing for those who have given their lives to the work of Christ.

It brings comfort for the suffering. The doctrine of Christ's coming brings hope to all who suffer for His name. Trials may press heavily upon us in this life, but they are not without purpose or reward. Peter reminds us in 1 Peter 4:12–13, "Beloved, think it not strange concerning the fiery trial which is to try you, as though some strange thing happened unto you: But rejoice, inasmuch as ye are partakers of Christ's sufferings; that, when his glory shall be revealed, ye may be glad also with exceeding joy."

Our sufferings, no matter how bitter, are but a precursor to the sweetness of that day. Consider the names given to the day of Christ's appearing: it is "the day of redemption," for we are sealed to it (Ephesians 4:30); it is the "day of the manifestation of the sons of God," when we shall be revealed in glory (1 John 3:2); and it is a "day of refreshing" in the presence of the Lord (Acts 3:19). The hardships we endure now, whether they be grief, persecution, or affliction, are eclipsed by the promise of eternal rest and glory. When Christ appears, we will be freed from all suffering and sorrow, and His glory will shine upon us forever.

Comfort for the misjudged. This doctrine is a balm to those of us who have been slandered, misrepresented, or unjustly condemned. How often are believers accused of things they never did or maligned simply for their faith? The world is quick to label hypocrites or fanatics for bearing a Bible or praying fervently, or even praying before a meal. Perhaps there have even been unjust rulings in courts of law or unfair judgments from those who should have been defended. But take heart: the day of Christ's coming will be a day of righteous judgment. Jude reminds us, "Behold, the Lord cometh with ten thousands of his saints, to execute judgment upon all," (Jude 14–15). This is the day Paul calls "the day of the revelation of the righteous judgment of God," (Romans 2:5). Every false accusation will be overturned, and every malicious word will be silenced. Christ will not only vindicate His people, but He will judge those who judged them unrighteously. On that day, the scales of justice will be balanced perfectly, and the truth will be revealed.

It will be a day of comfort for all believers. The day of the Lord is not a day to fear but a day to long for with eager hearts. It is the great culmination of all God's promises, the final unveiling of His redemptive work. For His people, it is the greatest day of freedom and joy. Though there may be weariness now, there is assurance that the Lord Himself will wipe away every tear and welcome His people into His presence with gladness.

So this doctrine calls for living with a steady hope (holy momentum), fixing eyes on Christ and the glory to be revealed. Let Paul's words be taken to heart: "Comfort one another with these words," (1

Thessalonians 4:18). Whether laboring in ministry, enduring suffering, or standing against the judgments of the world, there is solace in the knowledge that Christ is coming again.

The trumpet will sound, the dead will rise, and there will be a catching up to meet the Savior. On that day, the pain and trials of this life will fade like a passing shadow, replaced by the everlasting light of His glory. This is the hope, the joy, and the crown of rejoicing. Let it be clung to, for the day of the Lord will indeed be the greatest day ever.

Chapter 4:
Leave the World Behind

"And Jacob said, O God of my father Abraham, and God of my father Isaac, the LORD which saidst unto me, Return unto thy country, and to thy kindred, and I will deal well with thee: I am not worthy of the least of all the mercies, and of all the truth, which thou hast shewed unto thy servant; for with my staff I passed over this Jordan; and now I am become two bands," (Gen. 32:9–10).

The prayer of Jacob in Genesis 32:9–10 provides a glimpse into the soul of a man deeply aware of both his vulnerability and the majesty of the God he petitions. His words stand as a weighty reflection on the relationship between divine faithfulness and human insufficiency because of the fall. The scene unfolds with the patriarch standing on the precipice of a dangerous reunion with his estranged brother, Esau. Twenty years had passed since Jacob fled under the weight of deception and Esau's seething wrath. Now, with his household divided into camps and the promise of God ringing in his memory, Jacob's prayer rises like incense—honest, humble, and desperate.

Jacob's approach begins by anchoring himself in the history of the *covenant*: "O God of my father Abraham, and God of my father Isaac, the LORD which saidst unto me, Return unto thy country, and to thy kindred, and I will deal well with thee," (Genesis 32:9). This is no shallow plea; it is a deliberate invocation of the covenantal faithfulness of God. The patriarch identifies the Almighty as the One who walked with Abraham through deserts and promised Isaac descendants as numerous as the stars. By calling upon the God of his fathers, Jacob declares that he is not approaching a distant or impersonal deity but the covenant-keeping LORD who binds Himself by His own promises.

Jacob's acknowledgment of divine command reinforces his plea. When he paraphrases God's command to return as the Lord spoke to him, he demonstrates his obedience. Yet behind this statement lies a deeper implication—Jacob had not sought this path out of ambition or self-preservation but at the behest of divine instruction. He had left Haran not merely to reclaim a homeland but because God had commanded him to go. In his fear, Jacob's words serve as a subtle reminder that his obedience places the outcome of this reunion squarely in the hands of the Almighty.

Yet, it is in verse 10 where Jacob's prayer reaches its most vulnerable and introspective point: "I am not worthy of the least of all the mercies, and of all the truth, which thou hast showed unto thy servant; for with my staff I passed over this Jordan, and now I am become two bands." The Hebrew phrase "I am too small" (קָטֹנְתִּי *qāṭōnětî*) reveals more than a passing sentiment of humility. It captures the posture of a man who recognizes that he is entirely undeserving of God's steadfast kindness. This confession echoes the self-effacing words of other biblical figures who understood their low estate before the Almighty, being recipients of mercy at best. David confessed his insignificance when contemplating his royal lineage (2 Samuel 7:18). Jacob's use of this language signifies that his plea for deliverance rests not in any merit of his own but in the boundless mercy of God.

Jacob's reference to "all the mercies and all the truth" underscores the intensity of his acknowledgment. The plural form of "mercies" (חֲסָדִים *chasadim*) conveys an overwhelming abundance—acts of covenantal love that go beyond human comprehension. God's "truth" (אֱמֶת *emeth*) does not merely signify factuality but a faithfulness that upholds every promise made. Jacob acknowledges that the life he now lives is a testament to divine generosity. When he crossed the Jordan with nothing but his staff, he was a solitary wanderer. It was God and him. He left the world behind and went with God. Now, he stood as the head of a household so large that it could be split into two camps for safety. This transformation was a vivid emblem of God's fulfilled promise—a promise Jacob knew he could not have secured through his own devices.

This moment of reflection is not devoid of self-awareness. Though Jacob does not explicitly confess his deception regarding Esau and the blessing, his unworthiness hints at a recognition of past sins. The mention of himself as a "servant" before God mirrors the language he had used when addressing Esau (Genesis 32:4–5). It marks a posture of submission that he had once manipulated but now embraced sincerely. Such humility is not contrived; it is born from the realization that the preservation of his family and the fulfillment of the covenant could only be secured by God's grace.

In verse 11, Jacob's petition turns to a plea for deliverance: "Deliver me, I pray thee, from the hand of my brother, from the hand of Esau: for I fear him, lest he will come and smite me, and the mother with the children." The repetition of "from the hand" intensifies the urgency of his cry. It evokes the imagery of being caught within the grasp of an inescapable force. Jacob's ingenuity and resourcefulness had carried him far in life, but at this moment, he acknowledges his helplessness. The language of deliverance (נָצַל *nāṣal*) is a term frequently found in the Psalms, often used to describe rescue from overwhelming danger (Psalm 31:15; Psalm 59:1). Here, Jacob's use of it underscores his recognition that only divine intervention could preserve him and his household from ruin.

What makes this plea even more poignant is Jacob's honest confession of fear. This is not the posturing of a patriarch seeking to maintain a stoic demeanor; it is the voice of a man fully aware of the stakes. Esau's approach with four hundred men is not merely a family visit—to Jacob, it looms as an armed reckoning. Yet, even in voicing his fear, Jacob does not give way to despair. Instead, he anchors his prayer in the promise given at Bethel: "Thou saidst, I will surely do thee good, and make thy seed as the sand of the sea, which cannot be numbered for multitude," (Genesis 32:12).

Jacob's decision to quote God's own words is an act of holy faith (*holy momentum*). The patriarch is not reminding God out of doubt but out of trust—trust that God is bound by His unchanging character and covenant. The promise to multiply Jacob's descendants is not an abstract idea but a personal assurance that his children, though vulnerable, are safeguarded by divine decree. This reference to the promise evokes earlier covenantal imagery, recalling God's words to Abraham: "I will multiply thy seed as the stars of the heaven, and as the sand which is upon the sea shore," (Genesis 22:17). Jacob places his entire hope in the reality that what God has spoken cannot fail.

Yet, it is significant that Jacob's prayer ends without presumption. There is no demand, no assertion that he deserves a particular outcome. He places himself entirely at the mercy of God's providential care. Is this what Christians are to do? This lack of presumption marks the difference between entitlement and faith. While the text does not record God's immediate verbal response, the events that follow demonstrate that Jacob's prayer did not fall on deaf ears. In the unfolding narrative, the divine response comes not only in the peaceful meeting with Esau but in the mysterious wrestling match and prayer at Peniel, where Jacob learns that prevailing with God requires both surrender and strength.

In Jacob's prayer, the believer sees a mirror of the spiritual journey. The language of unworthiness resonates with every Christian who has come to terms with the weight of personal sin. The acknowledgment of divine mercy echoes the heart of those who remember seasons of desolation transformed by grace. And the cry for deliverance is the cry of every soul facing trials that seem insurmountable. Yet, as Jacob's prayer illustrates, the believer's hope lies not in human resilience but in the immutable promises of God. Just as Jacob clung to the words spoken to him, the Christian clings to the cross, where mercy and truth converge.

This prayer, filled with trembling yet anchored in faith, stands as a testament to the way God meets His people in their need—not always with the absence of fear, but with the assurance of His presence.

Doctrine: Going with God, Jacob only had a staff and left the world behind. Jacob's reflection in Genesis 32:10, "With my staff I passed over this Jordan," captures the essence of a journey that began with nothing but faith.[11] The staff in Jacob's hand was a symbol of both necessity and humility—he had no wealth, no servants, no possessions beyond what he could carry. The staff, a common tool of travelers and shepherds, represents his vulnerability as he ventured forward solely with God's promise as his guide. It marked the contrast between his empty-handed departure and his return with a vast household. This simple object—a staff—embodied Jacob's dependence. He had nothing else to lean on except for the literal and metaphorical support of God.

When Jacob fled from Esau's wrath, he left behind the comforts of his father's household, carrying no inheritance with him. His journey to Laban's house began in fear and uncertainty. The staff was his only tangible reminder of his frailty, yet it became a silent witness to God's faithfulness. In Scripture, the staff often represents trust amidst weakness. Just as Moses would later hold his staff as a sign of God's authority, Jacob's staff symbolized submission to God's guidance rather than his own strength. The act of taking his staff and crossing the Jordan without any provision showed that Jacob moved forward solely because of God's direction. His physical emptiness emphasized that every

---

[11] "What is faith?" A resting upon Christ alone for salvation." William Slatyer, *The Compleat Christian*, (London: Printed for the authour, 1643), 72. Or see Flavel, "Quest. 86. What is Faith in Jesus Christ? Answer. Faith in Iesus Christ is a saving Grace, whereby we receive and rest upon him alone for Salvation as he is offered to us in the Gospel." John Flavel, *An Exposition of the Assemblies Catechism*, (London: Printed for Tho. Cockerill, 1692), 162.

step of his journey was an act of faith. By mentioning the staff in his prayer, Jacob was acknowledging that from the very beginning, his survival and success were not the results of his own wisdom or cunning but of God's care. The staff also points to the broader truth that Jacob's journey was never truly solitary. Though he appeared alone, God's presence accompanied him at every turn. In Bethel, God reassured him with the vision of the heavenly ladder and angels ascending and descending—a powerful reminder that God was guiding his steps. The staff, though simple, became a reminder that Jacob's safety was never found in possessions or strength, but in the promise that God had made to him. His journey, taken with nothing more than his staff, was not a tale of human resilience but a testimony *to divine provision.*

Jacob's return to the Jordan with "two bands" further emphasizes this transformation. The same river he crossed in need now bore witness to his abundance, yet Jacob attributed none of this to his own effort. The contrast between "my staff" and the "two bands" is striking—it reflects the radical difference that God's blessings make. Jacob's prayer encapsulates the truth that it was God who upheld him, preserved him, and increased him. The staff stands as a symbol of surrender and trust, reminding believers that when they are called to walk into the unknown with seemingly nothing, God's promises will always sustain them. Jacob began with a staff, but he journeyed with God.

Jacob's declaration in Genesis 32:10, "With my staff I passed over this Jordan, and now I am become two bands," paints a vivid image of faith, humility, and dependence on God. The phrase "with my staff" signifies not merely a physical journey but a spiritual posture. Jacob entered the unknown without material wealth or earthly security, relying solely on God's promises. Jacob going with God only had a staff and left the world behind. This act of faith illustrates the believer's calling to forsake worldly reliance and lean entirely upon the providence and strength of God.

The imagery of a staff carries deep theological and symbolic weight in Scripture. A staff, in the biblical sense, is both a simple instrument and a powerful metaphor. It was commonly used as a walking aid for support during long journeys (Exodus 21:19), a symbol of God's pastoral care (Psalm 23:4), and a means of defense (1 Chronicles 11:23). The staff represents stability amidst uncertainty and weakness. For Jacob, the staff was the only possession he carried as he crossed the Jordan River. It served as a reminder of his human frailty and utter dependence on divine mercy. To go with a staff alone signifies entering life's trials without pomp or worldly might but with a heart set on the promises of God.

Jacob's journey began with nothing but his staff, yet it was marked by the presence and providence of the Almighty. Unlike Abraham's servant, who was sent with camels, gold, and gifts (Genesis 24:10), Jacob departed from Beersheba with only the bare necessities. The simplicity of his departure emphasizes the principle that God's call does not always include material abundance.

Instead, Jacob's staff pointed to the sufficiency of God's provision. When believers walk in obedience to God (*holy momentum*), though their external circumstances may appear impoverished, they carry the wealth of divine promises.

The staff also represents an emblem of submission. When Jacob acknowledges his unworthiness, saying, "I am not worthy of the least of all the mercies and of all the truth which thou hast showed unto thy servant," (Genesis 32:10), he exemplifies the posture of true humility. Christians must come before God recognizing their unworthiness and inability to claim any merit apart from His grace. In this way, Jacob's acknowledgment rebukes the presumption of self-sufficiency and calls for a dependence that mirrors the walk of Christ Himself, who "humbled himself and became obedient unto death," (Philippians 2:8).

The act of *leaning* upon the staff symbolizes spiritual reliance. Just as a weary traveler leans upon a staff for rest and balance, so too did Jacob lean upon the promises of God. This posture contrasts with the arrogance of the proud who presume, to walk alone without aid. Jacob's staff, therefore, is a representation of a life upheld by divine strength rather than human ambition. This truth aligns with the teaching of Psalm 23:4: "Thy rod and thy staff, they comfort me." The rod of God's guidance and the staff of His protection sustain the believer in every season of trial.

Jacob's journey also teaches an important lesson about how God magnifies His faithfulness. When Jacob fled from his home, he was impoverished, vulnerable, and alone. Years later, he returned with flocks, herds, and a household divided into two bands—a visible testament to God's blessing and faithfulness. This transformation from poverty to abundance was not the result of Jacob's cunning but of divine providence. God's care for Jacob displays His covenant faithfulness, showing that when believers entrust their lives to Him, He is able to do "exceeding abundantly above all that they ask or think," (Ephesians 3:20).

In Jacob's confession, the believer sees a rejection of entitlement and an embrace of gratitude. The statement, "I am not worthy of the least of all the mercies," demonstrates that Jacob understood the depth of God's grace. Christians, likewise, must recognize that every blessing—whether material or spiritual—is an unmerited gift from a benevolent Father. Murmuring against God's providence reflects a failure to acknowledge His goodness. As Jacob acknowledges his unworthiness, he models the necessity of contentment in both lack and abundance.

The staff also points forward to the New Testament, where Christ instructs His disciples to carry "nothing for their journey, save a staff only," (Mark 6:8). This directive reinforces the principle that those sent by God are to walk by faith and not by sight. The apostles, like Jacob, were called to lean wholly upon divine provision rather than material security. This connection underscores the continuity of God's purposes throughout redemptive history. Faithful servants of God have always been called to renounce the world's riches and walk according to the Spirit.

Jacob's staff also reminds believers of the necessity of perseverance. The journey across the Jordan was not the end but the beginning of a path marked by trials and divine encounters. Jacob would wrestle with the angel of the Lord, have his name changed to Israel, and bear a limp as a perpetual reminder of his dependence on God. The staff, once a symbol of simplicity, became an emblem of a life shaped by God's sovereign hand. Christians must remember that the walk of faith often involves seasons of hardship that test and refine. It is through these seasons that believers come to know God as their true refuge and strength.

Furthermore, Jacob's testimony calls believers to reflect on their own spiritual journey. Many begin their walk with Christ with few earthly possessions but the promise of eternal life. Over time, God may choose to bless some with material wealth, while others continue in humble circumstances. Yet, regardless of external conditions, the true inheritance of believers is found in Christ, who is "the same yesterday, and today, and forever," (Hebrews 13:8). The believer's treasure is not stored in earthly storehouses but in the eternal promises secured by the blood of the Lamb.

The example of Jacob's journey also rebukes the pride that so easily ensnares the human heart. When Christians forget their initial dependence on God, they may be tempted to attribute their success to their own efforts. Jacob's declaration stands as a guardrail against such thinking. When he says, "with my staff I passed over this Jordan," he reminds believers that all progress and prosperity come from the Lord. Every achievement and blessing must be received with humility and used for God's glory.

Ultimately, the narrative of Jacob and his staff points to the faithfulness of God. The world offers false security in wealth, reputation, and power, but these things cannot uphold the soul in times of trial. Only God's promises endure. The believer is called to walk by faith, leaning on the divine staff of God's unchanging Word. As Jacob returned to the land of promise with testimony of God's provision, so too will believers enter their heavenly inheritance with praise for the faithfulness of their Redeemer. By abandoning worldly trust and walking in holiness, believers echo the words of the psalmist: "The Lord is my portion," (Psalm 16:5).

Jacob's staff, therefore, serves as a powerful reminder that the Christian life is not sustained by human effort but by divine grace. Every step of the journey, from the barren Jordan to the place of blessing, is directed by the hand of God. Believers are called to forsake worldly reliance, lean wholly upon their Savior, and live according to the promises that find their fulfillment in Christ. The life of faith is one of simplicity, perseverance, and unwavering trust in the God who brings His people safely home.

The Christian who truly walks with God perceives the comforts of this life as temporary and incapable of satisfying the soul's deepest longings. While grateful for daily provisions, even the simplest, the believer does not cling to earthly comforts but stands ready to release them whenever God wills. Jacob's humility in saying, "I am less than the least of all Thy mercies," exemplifies this heart posture. Like the primitive Christians who joyfully endured the loss of all they had, a believer desires not worldly gain but the presence of God. Paul's longing to depart and be with Christ demonstrates how faith elevates the soul above earthly attachments.

The blessings God gives can be categorized as either *temporal or spiritual.* Temporal blessings—such as health, provision, and stability—come from His providence. Yet they are limited and perishable, serving only the physical body, which will return to dust. These temporal gifts, though good, are fraught with snares. Relationships, possessions, riches, and honors often distract the heart from God, dull spiritual senses, and hinder godly pursuits. Christians who become entangled in worldly pleasures find themselves weighed down, unable to serve God with fervor. It requires great wisdom to use such blessings without being ensnared by them. Believers must receive them with caution and gratitude while keeping their hearts detached from their allure.

Spiritual blessings, however, are the precious comforts that flow directly from God's Spirit through the means of grace—His Word, prayer, and worship. These include glimpses of heavenly joy, moments of weighty communion with Christ, and the witness of the Holy Spirit's love. David testified that "one day in Thy courts is better than a thousand elsewhere." Yet even these spiritual experiences, though sweet, are fleeting and incomplete in this life. The believer often struggles with spiritual dryness, distracted thoughts, and a sense of distance from God. Sometimes, despite earnest seeking, God seems hidden, leaving the soul longing for His presence.

This incompleteness stirs a holy desire in the believer to leave the transient comforts of this world behind and seek the fullness of eternal communion with Christ. Love, being an uniting affection, compels the soul toward its beloved, yearning for an unbroken, face-to-face fellowship with God. The believer longs to exchange the dim reflections of God seen through earthly ordinances for the perfect, radiant vision of Him in glory.

Christians, having seen God's salvation, like Jacob, need not fear death. For the redeemed, death is a conquered enemy, defeated by Christ's resurrection. Death, once a terror, has become a passage to eternal rest. It no longer separates the soul from God but unites the believer with Him. The Apostle Paul could declare, "O death, where is thy sting?" because in Christ, death has been disarmed and transformed into a gateway to everlasting life.

Therefore, leaving the world behind is not a loss but a *gain* for the believer. Earthly blessings, though good, pale in comparison to the eternal inheritance prepared by God. In heaven, there are no interruptions to joy, no sorrow, and no fear—only fullness of life in God's presence. The fleeting pleasures of this world cannot compare to the eternal, weighty glory that awaits. The believer, in contemplating this, grows increasingly willing to forsake all for the unshakable joy of being with Christ forever.

In this way, the call to leave the world behind is not a denial of God's good gifts but a pursuit (*holy momentum*) of something infinitely greater. The soul that loves God above all else recognizes that earthly comforts, though sweet, are fleeting shadows of a far greater reality. True faith propels believers to seek not merely the blessings of the journey but the unending joy of the destination—eternal life in the presence of their Savior. "How many adhere to Christ in Profession, and yet adhere to the world, or lust in Affection? Are there not many, who seem to recumb and lean on Christ for life, but yet really recumb, and lean upon self?"[12]

Will you leave the world behind and lean on the staff of Christ? Jacob's life reminds us of the necessity of leaning on God as he leaned on his staff—choosing faith over fear, trust over self-reliance, and God's promises over the comforts of the world. As believers, we are called to follow this pattern, understanding that God's leading brings both comfort and correction. The staff symbolizes His power and provision, reminding us that His faithfulness sustains us in every trial.

When Jacob crossed the Jordan with only his staff, he showed that reliance on God begins with surrender. Believers must recognize that strength and security do not come from earthly possessions or status. The "staff" must be the Word of God—the true foundation and guide. Psalm 23 assures that God's rod and staff comfort His people. His rod is His Word of direction, while His staff represents His protection and correction.

---

[12] Theophilus Gale, *Christ's Tears for Jerusalems Unbelief and Ruine*, (London: printed for M. Widdowes at the Green Dragon in St. Pauls Church-Yard, 1679), 234.

As Christians, the question must be asked: is there a leaning on His Word daily, or a clinging to the false securities of this world? Jacob's example calls for loosening the grip on worldly comforts and distractions. He walked humbly, bearing no earthly wealth, trusting that God's promises were sufficient. There must be a willingness to leave behind what weighs down. Hebrews 12:1 calls for laying aside every weight—those sins and burdens that hinder the walk with Christ.

The world's honors, pleasures, and treasures can subtly become snares to the soul. Riches, positions of power, and the praise of men often entangle the heart, dulling affections for God. If there is a consuming desire to maintain these things, there is the danger of becoming like those who resisted Christ's reign and faced His rod of judgment (Psalm 2:9). Instead, there must be the resolve, like Jacob, to say, "Take the world, but give me Jesus."

Even when Jacob feared for his life before meeting Esau, he prayed for deliverance, confessing his unworthiness yet leaning on God's faithfulness. Fear often rises, yet there must be resting in God's promises. A person's resting on the promises is seen in the way they pray.

Prayer is the lifeline of the Christian life—a divine ordinance through which believers commune with the Almighty and are strengthened for their pilgrimage. As the psalmist declares, "Blessed is the man that maketh the LORD his trust," (Psalm 40:4). In prayer, there is an approach to the throne of grace in humility and faith, seeking not only deliverance but also the grace to persevere in holiness. Prayer must be both private and public, for Scripture commands prayer in the congregation (Psalm 40:9–10) and in the secret place of the heart, as Christ Himself taught: "Enter into thy closet, and...pray to thy Father which is in secret," (Matthew 6:6).

To pray effectively, there must be an approach to God according to the conditions laid out in Scripture. In faith without doubting: "Let him ask in faith, nothing wavering" (James 1:6). Faith anchors prayer, ensuring that petitions rest on the certainty of God's promises rather than wavering in unbelief.

In zeal and fervency: "The effectual fervent prayer of a righteous man availeth much," (James 5:16). Prayer must come from the depths of the heart.

In constancy and patience: "I waited patiently for the LORD; and he inclined unto me, and heard my cry," (Psalm 40:1). There must be persistence in prayer, trusting God's timing and resting in His perfect will.
In humility: "I am not worthy of the least of all the mercies," (Genesis 32:10). There must be abasement before God, acknowledging unworthiness.

With thanksgiving: "Bless the LORD, O my soul: and all that is within me, bless his holy name," (Psalm 103:1). Gratitude must accompany every request.

Renewing vows and promises: "I will pay my vows unto the LORD now in the presence of all his people," (Psalm 116:18). Prayer is an opportunity to reaffirm dedication to God.

With strong cries and groanings: Daniel cried for mercy, confessing both personal and national sin (Daniel 9:19). Prayer must echo with contrition and intercession.

With submission to God's will: "Thy will be done," (Matthew 26:42). True prayer bows to the sovereignty of God, trusting His wisdom in the matter, manner, and timing of every answer.

In all these, the believer is called to leave the world behind, lean wholly upon Christ, and walk forward (*holy momentum*) sustained not by self, but by the faithful hand of God.

The benefits of such prayer are manifold. Firstly, prayer strengthens believers in the grace of perseverance. Jesus said to Peter, "I have prayed for thee, that thy faith fail not," (Luke 22:32). Secondly, prayer keeps the Christian life vibrant and empowered. "Put on the whole armour of God...praying always with all prayer and supplication in the Spirit," (Ephesians 6:11, 18). Through prayer, the believer becomes vigilant, ready to resist temptation and to withstand spiritual attacks.

Moreover, prayer deepens fellowship with God. "Ye have received the Spirit of adoption, whereby we cry, Abba, Father," (Romans 8:15). This intimacy assures the soul of its standing in Christ and nurtures a sense of belonging to the heavenly family. Prayer also supplies daily needs, as James assures: "If any of you lack wisdom, let him ask of God...and it shall be given him," (James 1:5). Even in seasons of weakness, there is the echo of Paul's confidence: "My grace is sufficient for thee: for my strength is made perfect in weakness," (2 Corinthians 12:9).

Through prayer, temptations are subdued. When Jesus was tempted in the wilderness, He overcame through Scripture and steadfast prayer (Matthew 4:1–11). Prayer sanctifies daily life, turning ordinary moments into opportunities for worship. "For every creature of God is good, and nothing to be refused, if it be received with thanksgiving" (1 Timothy 4:4).

Prayer *prepares* the believer for eternity. "For I know that this shall turn to my salvation through your prayer, and the supply of the Spirit of Jesus Christ," (Philippians 1:19). Prayer aligns the heart with God's purposes and fixes the soul on the heavenly home where Christ reigns. It cultivates in believers a readiness to meet their Savior face to face, having walked closely with Him in prayer throughout their earthly pilgrimage. Prayer is not a mere duty but a privilege that strengthens, sustains, and sanctifies. As the pattern of Jacob is followed, who leaned on his staff and called upon the name of the Lord, there must be a walking humbly and fervently with God, laying all cares before

Him with the assurance that He is faithful to hear and to answer according to His perfect will. "The eyes of the LORD are upon the righteous, and his ears are open unto their cry," (Psalm 34:15).

Jacob leaned on his staff, so, in a metaphorical way, Christians must lean on Christ to walk with God. They lean on their staff and leave the world behind, going with God. In Christ, there is never separation from God's love (Romans 8:38–39). Jacob's journey was one of faith—leaving behind earthly securities to embrace the unseen promise of God. In the same way, there is a calling to live as pilgrims, seeking a better country (Hebrews 11:16). The pleasures of this world, though appealing, are fleeting. Only in God's presence is there "fullness of joy" and "pleasures forevermore," (Psalm 16:11).

Jacob's narrative also warns of the necessity of spiritual vigilance. Some submit to His grace and some resist His authority. There must be a clinging to Christ's scepter of righteousness rather than facing His rod of justice. As Christians, there must be living with eyes fixed on Christ, the Author and Finisher of faith. Just as Jacob leaned on his staff and trusted in God's faithfulness, there must be a daily leaning on Christ—the true Shepherd of souls. The journey may be filled with hardships, but His rod protects, corrects, and comforts. As the distractions of this world are left behind, there must be pressing forward to the promise of eternal joy in His presence.

There must be faithfulness—leaning on God's Word and trusting in His provision. And when the time comes to depart, there must be the full assurance to say, "I have seen God's salvation, and I am ready to be with Him."

One other question rises as a use: is there an approach to Him with the humility required for Him to listen? Unlike Jacob, there is often a lack of serious reflection upon personal unworthiness and frailty before commencing requests. This failure leads to irreverence and presumption—the very ruin of true prayer.

Some will pray and there is the faint, fearful, and distrustful prayer—a prayer that barely emerges, much less ascends. It sticks in the throat, unable to rise due to fear and doubt.

There is the cold, formal, and superficial prayer. This is what *most* people do. This prayer may be spoken clearly enough but lacks life and spirit. It freezes midway, failing to reach God's presence because it is devoid of fervor. "The effectual fervent prayer of a righteous man availeth much," (James 5:16). Cold prayers *always freeze* before they reach heaven.

There is also the bold, proud, and presumptuous prayer. This prayer shoots upward swiftly but is struck down just as quickly, as it presents itself arrogantly before God. Instead of receiving a blessing, it returns burdened with a curse. Such was the prayer of the Pharisee, described by our Lord: "The Pharisee stood and prayed thus with himself," (Luke 18:10). Although he entered the temple to pray, he had no request to offer. Instead of humbly confessing his unworthiness like Jacob, he offered what he considered a sacrifice of praise—praise for his own merits rather than praise for God's mercy. He rehearsed his good deeds, not to strengthen faith but as though to remind God of supposed worthiness.

There are instances in Scripture where even God's faithful servants—Hezekiah, Nehemiah, Job, and others—mention the sincerity of their hearts and their efforts for God's glory. Yet, when their prayers are compared to that of the Pharisee, there is a vast difference in tone and spirit. The prayers of the righteous bear no resemblance to the arrogant boasting of the self-righteous. The former offer humble, necessary affirmations, sometimes as a defense against accusation or to strengthen trust in God's promises. The latter are full of pride, scorn, and self-congratulation.

In this way, even when there is occasion to mention sincerity in prayer, it must be done in the same spirit of humility as the saints of old. There must be a guarding against pressing presumptuously into God's presence, lest there be, as Jacob feared, the bringing of a curse instead of a blessing (Genesis 27:12). Instead, there must be an *approach* to God with reverence, considering

His incomparable majesty and personal unworthiness. When there is a clear sight of the vast difference between His holiness and human vileness, prayers, seasoned with humility, will ascend freely to God and return with His gracious answer.

Hearts must bow low when entering the celestial court, where the King of kings reigns, surrounded by hosts of angelic beings. How shall a creature of dust and ashes approach such glory without humility, reverence, and fear? Thomas Gattaker said, "The lower we bow, the higher our prayers will rise." "A godly life, and a life of faith, are the same."[13] The church finds solace in leaning upon Christ. Jacob's staff is more than a walking stick—it is a declaration of trust in the Almighty. It is the symbol of the man who left the world behind, with nothing in his hand but faith in his heart. It is the same leaning that is seen in the beloved of the Song of Solomon: "Who is this that cometh up from the wilderness, leaning upon her beloved?" (Song of Solomon 8:5). That picture tells the whole story of faith. It is the story of a believer who has tried the world in a fallen state, found it wanting, been renewed in Christ, and cast off the world for the eternal embrace of Christ.

---

[13] Thomas Gouge, *The Young Man's Guide through the Wilderness of This World to the Heavenly Canaan Shewing Him How to Carry Himself Christian-like in the Whole Course of His Life*, (London: S. and B.G. for Nevil Simmons .., 1676), 114.

Now, let's be plain about it: leaning is not weakness—it is wisdom. Only a fool trusts himself when he is stumbling. Leaning comes from knowing who upholds. Jacob leaned on his staff not because he was infirm, but because he was wise enough to know that self-reliance is a lie. The world had stripped him down to his bare bones—gone were the comforts of home, the deceitful safety of riches, and the illusions of self-sufficiency. But what the world takes away, God fills with His presence. When Jacob passed over the Jordan with nothing but his staff, he was not poor—he was held.

So, what does it mean to lean on Christ? It means throwing the whole weight—body, soul, and spirit—onto Him. It means coming to terms with the fact that no one can save themselves, no matter how fiercely there is a striving to stand upright on one's own two feet. Jesus Himself calls to the weary, saying, "Come unto me, all ye that labour and are heavy laden, and I will give you rest," (Matthew 11:28). This is not a temporary reprieve—it is the soul's everlasting rest in the arms of the Beloved.

The beloved of the Song of Solomon leans because she trusts *completely*. She leans because she knows His strength *will not fail*. This is Christ, the Rock of Ages, the Cornerstone that holds the whole structure together (1 Peter 2:6). Why is there faltering? Is His hand too short that it cannot save? "I know whom I have believed," said Paul, "and am persuaded that he is able to keep that which I have committed unto him against that day," (2 Timothy 1:12).

But make no mistake—leaning on Christ does not merely mean trusting Him when the storms rage. It means handing over the reins *entirely*. Faith is not merely persuasion—it is surrender. It is standing in the wilderness, leaning on the Beloved, while the world sneers at dependence and mocks simplicity. But what they do not know is that His strength is made perfect in weakness (2 Corinthians 12:9).

What does this leaning look like? It looks like a soul saying, "Take what You will, Lord, give what You will. I am Yours." Faith parts with its dearest sins and says, "Let them go if they keep me from You." Faith kneels before the throne and whispers, "I have chosen You for my portion. Whatever comes, there is contentment in Your hands." And what follows is this: the soul no longer fears the wilderness or the shadow of death. Leaning on the Beloved means there is nothing to dread, for "perfect love casteth out fear," (1 John 4:18).

This is why the Church finds refuge and joy in *leaning* on Christ. His arms are strong enough to carry burdens and tender enough to embrace fears. When there is leaning on Him, there is not merely safety—there is home. And when home is found in Christ, there is a walking through the valley of weeping and a coming out singing. Cross the Jordan with a stick.

This is the beauty of leaning on the Beloved: the world fades, the burdens lift, and there is strengthening with a peace that the world cannot give and cannot take away.

So, let the world scorn dependence if it will. Let them laugh at faith as a crutch. But when the storms come and the winds howl, the believer, like Jacob, will still be standing—because there has been a learning that the safest place to be is leaning on the everlasting arms.

Chapter 5:
Loving Things Unseen

"Whom having not seen, ye love; in whom, though now ye see him not, yet believing, ye rejoice with joy unspeakable and full of glory," (1 Peter 1:8).

It is a strange thing for anyone to speak of love for something *unseen*. If someone were to sit on the edge of a dock and tell a passing fisherman that they adored a captain they had never laid eyes on, the fisherman might tilt his head and wonder if the person had spent too long in the sun. After all, the world trains affections through the senses. People believe what they see, trust what they can touch, and invest in what their hands can grasp. Yet, Peter calls attention to a reality that defies the ordinary rules of engagement—a love born not from sight but from faith. This is not a blind faith. It is a faith that is set in the reality of God's self-revelation to His people.

Here in 1 Peter 1:8, the apostle marvels at a relationship with Christ that bypasses the eyes yet grips the mind and affects the heart. Peter writes about people who are well-acquainted with suffering. Their belief cost them dearly. These Christians in Asia Minor endured ridicule, exile, and loss, all because of their love for a Savior they had never seen. "Whom having not seen, ye love," Peter declares,. acknowledging the remarkable nature of such love. In Paul's time, gods were plastered in temple alcoves and emperors paraded their might for all to see, but to love an unseen Christ was both a scandal and a wonder at the same time.

Peter's language in this verse drips with admiration. The Greek participle for "seeing" (ἰδόντες *idontes*) is in the aorist tense, indicating a completed action—a sight never granted to these believers. And yet, the verb "to love" (ἀγαπάω *agapaō*) stands resolutely in the present. Their love does not depend on an eyewitness account but on something deeper, stronger—a divine revelation grasped by faith. Here is where interest in this verse unfolds: things unseen can be loved because faith makes the invisible more vivid than the things that are seen.

This is no sentimental notion. Peter does not hand out hollow platitudes. He knows what he is commending. Faith in the unseen Christ binds people to an inheritance "incorruptible, and undefiled, and that fadeth not away," (1 Peter 1:4). This inheritance is guarded not by human strength but by God's almighty power. Such faith surpasses the need for sight because it grips a reality more solid than stone.

The question arises: How does a person come to love what they have never seen? One might think of how a child loves the stories of a father long gone—clinging to every tale passed down by their mother, building affection on the sturdy ground of memory and promise.

But Christ offers something even richer than

memory; He offers His presence through faith in the Word. The believers Peter describes do not rely on secondhand accounts alone. Their faith is active, and their hearts are alive with the joy of anticipation.

Peter introduces another participle, "not seeing now" (ἄρτι μὴ ὁρῶντες *arti mē horōntes*), pointing to the present moment. The absence of Christ's physical form does not lessen their belief. Instead, Peter commends their persistent trust despite ongoing trials. This trust is not a passive state but an active, deliberate confidence in Christ's promises—the kind that withstands the "fiery trials" described earlier in the chapter (1 Peter 1:7).

There is a grand theological truth here: sight is *not* the highest form of knowledge (at least from an earthly perspective). Peter follows in the footsteps of Jesus, who declared to Thomas, "Blessed are they that have not seen, and yet have believed," (John 20:29). In Scripture, sight is often portrayed as the reward for faith, not its foundation. Moses endured "as seeing him who is invisible," (Hebrews 11:27), and the writer of Hebrews insists that "faith is the substance of things hoped for, the evidence of things not seen," (Hebrews 11:1). To demand sight before faith is to misunderstand the very nature of Christian belief.

The people Peter speaks of believed in Christ's promises of redemption, resurrection, and glory. Though they did not see Him during His earthly ministry, they experienced Him in their conversion, in the community of believers, and in moments of joy amid sorrow. Their belief was not abstract. It was as real to them as the stones beneath their feet and the sky above their heads. This faith produces joy, but not an ordinary happiness that shifts with the winds of circumstance. Peter uses a word (ἀγαλλιᾶσθε *agalliasthē*) that conveys an exuberant, almost overwhelming joy. This is not the polite smile of someone trying to appear content. It is the uncontainable exultation of someone who has found treasure. And this joy, Peter says, is "ἀνεκλάλητος *aneklaletos*"—inexpressible. Human language falters before the weight of such glory.

Peter does not stop at joy. He adds that this joy is "δεδοξασμένη *dedoxasmenē*"—glorified. This word, often reserved for divine splendor, emphasizes that a believer's joy is infused with the brilliance of God's glory. It is a joy that anticipates the final revelation of Christ and mirrors the radiance of heaven itself.

Why, then, this repetition of the unseen? Why does Peter return to the idea of not seeing Christ? The shift from "not having seen" to "not seeing now" shows the temporal tension of the Christian life. People live in the "already and not yet." They are already redeemed, already heirs of the kingdom, yet they await the full consummation of that inheritance. Their joy is anchored in a future certainty so vivid that it bleeds into their present reality.

The brilliance of Peter's exhortation lies in how he redefines the very notion of *seeing*. What the natural eye cannot perceive, the eye of faith beholds by the Word and through the Spirit. This redefinition elevates love from mere sentiment to a supernatural act of worship. It is a love that defies the natural order, for it clings to a Person whose presence is grasped by faith and not by sight.

This love for the unseen Christ also serves as a defining mark of the Christian community. In the Old Testament, love for God was the hallmark of Israel's identity: "Thou shalt love the Lord thy God with all thine heart," (Deuteronomy 6:5). Peter draws on this covenantal language and applies it to the love people have for Christ. This love is not abstract piety; it is covenant loyalty. Just as Israel was called to love the God they could not see but knew through His works and promises, the Church loves Christ through the testimony of His resurrection and the promise of His return.

Peter's focus on love and belief also links back to Jesus' farewell discourse: "He that hath my commandments, and keepeth them, he it is that loveth me," (John 14:21). Love for Christ, born out of faith, produces obedience. These early Christians did not simply claim belief; they lived it. Their faith was not a theoretical exercise but a reality manifested in their suffering and joy.

In reflecting on 1 Peter 1:8, there must be a reckoning with this truth: things unseen can be loved, but things unknown cannot be loved. To know Christ is to love Him, even if He has never been seen. Affection for Him grows as people learn of His character, His works, and His promises. Just as one cannot love a stranger, neither can anyone love Christ apart from knowing Him. But in knowing Him through His Word, His Spirit, and His community, hearts are stirred with a love that does *not* require sight.

This passage invites examination of the nature of faith. Is there belief because it is convenient or because it is true? Is there rejoicing in the unseen Christ with a joy that confounds the world? Peter's words press the soul to live as one who sees beyond the veil of this life to the eternal glory to come. Love for Christ, unseen yet known, becomes the anthem of faith, declaring that the invisible is more precious than anything the eye can behold.

And anyone that does not have this threefold power of believing, of loving, and of rejoicing in Christ, does not know Christ.

Doctrine: things unseen can be loved because faith makes the invisible more vivid than the things that are seen.

The duty and defining characteristic of a true Christian is to love the Lord Jesus Christ, even though they have never seen Him. What is this love? This love is not mere sentiment but a genuine and active devotion rooted in faith. True Christians are described as chosen by God, sanctified by the Holy Spirit, and set apart for obedience. Their election is not random but part of God's eternal purpose, making them vessels of honor in His service.

This sanctification affects the whole person—their thoughts, will, affections, and actions. Their understanding is enlightened, their desires are directed toward heavenly things, and even their bodies become instruments of righteousness. Their obedience flows from the grace they have received, demonstrating their love for Christ.

Loving an unseen Savior requires a faith that surpasses the need for sight, rooted in Christ's promises and His redeeming work. This love sets true Christians apart, marked by holiness, joy, and loyalty to their Redeemer (a fueling of *holy momentum*). "The Life of Christianity consists very much in our love to Christ. Without love to Christ, we are as much without spiritual life, as a carcass when the Soul is fled from it, is without natural life. Faith without Love to Christ, is a dead Faith; and a Christian without Love to Christ, is a dead Christian; dead in sins and trespasses."[14]

The object of a true Christian's love is Jesus Christ, whom they have never seen. This Jesus is the

---

[14] Thomas Vincent, *The True Christians Love of the Unseen Christ*, (London: J.R. for Samuel Sprint, 1677), 1–2.

eternal Son of God, the second Person of the Trinity, who took on human nature and walked among humanity in mortal flesh. He lived humbly, died a criminal's death on the cross for sin, and rose on the third day for justification. After forty days, He ascended to heaven, where He intercedes for believers and prepares a place for them in His Father's house.

Jesus is called "Savior" because He redeems people from their sins (Matthew 1:21) and "Christ" because He is anointed as Prophet, Priest, and King. While some early Christians, like Paul and Stephen, saw Him in visions, no believer today has seen His glorified body. Instead, they know Him through His Word, the sacraments, and His image reflected in fellow believers. Yet, it is this unseen Jesus who captivates their love.

The fact that Christ will demonstrate His love to those who *love Him* is one of the most comforting promises in Scripture. Jesus declared that those who keep His commandments and love Him will experience His love and the love of the Father, along with a personal manifestation of Himself. "He that hath my commandments, and keepeth them, he it is that loveth me: and he that loveth me shall be loved of my Father, and I will love him, and will manifest myself to him," (John 14:21). This manifestation is not a physical vision but a spiritual unveiling of His glory and love to them.

Christ reveals Himself by deepening the believer's understanding of His beauty and character through the Spirit of wisdom and revelation. This is more than intellectual knowledge—it is a heart-level awareness that enlivens faith and strengthens the soul. Sometimes, this manifestation involves a renewed sense of Christ's nearness, filling the believer's heart with peace and joy amid trials.

At the heart of this revelation is the assurance of Christ's *unchanging love*. In moments of spiritual darkness, when His presence feels distant, His eventual revelation feels like the morning light after a long night. His Spirit speaks inwardly, assuring the soul: "I am your Savior. You are mine forever." This sweet communion fills believers with inexpressible joy, reminding them that no earthly delight compares to knowing Christ's love and anticipating the day when they will see Him face to face.

This is what Peter was stressing in his letter. Equally true, things unseen may be loved, but things unknown cannot be loved. God sets spiritual realities before believers, not only through the Bible's revelation but also by bringing these truths to the touchpoint of their spiritual senses. Faith opens the eyes of the heart to see the unseen. Believers have tasted heaven's sweetness through communion with God, much like travelers sampling treasures from distant lands they have never visited. As the Apostle John declared, "That which our eyes have seen and our hands have handled," believers can affirm that God has placed the first fruits of His promises in their hands.

The joy of the Lord lingers on the soul's palate, confirming the unseen realities of heaven. Hebrews 10:34 recalls how early believers endured loss joyfully, knowing they possessed a better inheritance above. This experiential knowledge surpasses secondhand reports. When Peter wrote, "Whom having not seen, ye love," he captured the mystery of loving an unseen Savior with joy unspeakable. There is far more of heaven tasted in this life than most are aware.

Yet, many believers live beneath the joy and comfort available to them because they do not know the Word of God's self-revelation very well at all.

While deep communion with God is attainable, many remain at the base of the mountain, caught between hope and fear. Their spiritual homes are impoverished, missing the riches of assurance. Why? The distractions of the world often drown out heavenly thoughts. Believers become entangled in earthly concerns, leaving little time for communion with God. How easily the noise of life mutes the soul's spiritual hunger.

Formality creeps into religious duties, starving the heart of its vitality. Routine can become like ivy choking a tree, binding and weakening the believer's spiritual growth. True communion with God cannot thrive where faith becomes mere habit. This is not the movement of *holy momentum.*

Persistent temptations weigh on the mind, especially for those prone to melancholy or despair. Such struggles often leave believers weary, unable to draw comfort from their devotions in the Word.

The decay of first love *dampens* spiritual fervor and holy momentum. Revelation 2:4 warns against forsaking one's initial passion for Christ. They are not to forget their first love. When duty is performed with coldness rather than love, the heart's joy diminishes.

And spiritual pride can easily undermine comfort. Like strong wine in weak vessels (Matt. 9:17), the joys of the Spirit can be overwhelming. Pride distorts humility, making believers unable to rest fully in God's grace.

These hindrances reveal why many believers miss the fullness of joy offered to them. Faith invites believers not just to hear of Christ's promises but to taste and experience them, embracing a hidden life of assurance and communion with the unseen yet ever-present Savior.

Sincere Christians love this invisible Christ because of His unmatched loveliness, perceived not by the body's eye, but by the eye of faith through the Word. Scripture provides vivid descriptions of Christ's beauty. Do they ponder and consider them?

In Song of Solomon 5:9, the daughters of Jerusalem inquire of the bride, "What is thy beloved more than another beloved?" In response, the bride extols Christ's surpassing beauty, declaring Him "white and ruddy, the chief among ten thousand," and concluding with the profound affirmation, "Yea, He is altogether lovely." This exalted language points to Christ's excellence in every regard.

Though believers cannot see Him personally standing before them, Christ's loveliness is evident in His person and covenant work (he is fully revealed in the word and is all glorious within it). His human nature, comprising body and soul, was glorious even in humility and now radiates divine splendor in exaltation. Philippians 3:21 calls His risen body a "glorious body." If Moses' face shone after mere communion on Mount Sinai, how much more radiant is Christ's body after ascending to the heavenly Mount Zion. His glorified humanity outshines all visible creation.

Yet, His soul's beauty surpasses even this. Christ embodies perfect holiness, wisdom, and compassion. In His earthly ministry, He excelled in virtue beyond all who ever lived—meekness greater than Moses, wisdom surpassing Solomon, and patience exceeding Job. Now enthroned in heaven, His excellence surpasses the perfected spirits of the redeemed and even the splendor of the sinless angels. While creatures display beams of wisdom and sparks of holiness, Christ is the source—

the sun from which all rays shine. In Him is the fullness of the Spirit without measure (John 3:34).

Christ's divine nature deepens His glory immeasurably. As God, He shares the Father's eternal glory. He declared, "I AM," (John 8:28), signifying His unchanging and infinite being. Scripture calls Him the "Lord of Glory," (1 Corinthians 2:8), and the "King of Glory," (Psalm 24:7). When Christ ascended, heaven's gates were lifted for His triumphal entry, as He took His place at the *right hand* of the Father.

Paul's description of Christ in Colossians 1:15–19 emphasizes His glorious supremacy: "the image of the invisible God, the firstborn of every creature," the Creator and sustainer of all things. He is before all things and holds all things together. He is the head of the church and the firstborn from the dead, embodying preeminence in all things.

This unmatched beauty draws believers *irresistibly*. They love Him not only because of His divine authority but because of His grace, wisdom, and mercy. His words are sweeter than honey—His doctrine, precepts, and promises surpass every earthly delight. Unlike the most admired human beings, who have flaws, Christ is "altogether lovely," untainted by imperfection. The Christian life involves beholding Christ's glory through faith in the doctrines of the Word and longing for the day when this faith becomes sight. Though hidden from physical eyes, Christ's beauty fills the soul with a love stronger than death. This unseen yet ever-present Savior captivates believers because He is not only their Lord but their Beloved Friend.

In this love to Christ, all true believers possess an unshakable foundation for rejoicing (a kind of *derivative* of holy momentum), as the apostle says, "...ye rejoice with joy unspeakable," (1 Peter 1:8). Their joy is rooted not in fleeting circumstances, but in Christ's enduring promises and His self-revelation to them. Even in trials, they rejoice, for faith opens the heart to His unseen beauty, turning grief into hope and filling their souls with inexpressible gladness. "The spiritual joy and heavenly comfort which the peace and grace of God ministers to the consciences of believers, Rom. 15:13; 5:1; Phil. 4:4; 1 Pet. 1:8, is said to make the 'bones flourish like an herb,' Isa. 66:14. (As, on the other side, of 'a broken spirit' it is said, that it 'drieth the bones,' Prov. 17:22.) 'Their soul' (saith the prophet) 'shall be as a watered garden; and they shall not sorrow any more. I will turn their mourning into joy, and will comfort them, and make them rejoice from their sorrow,' Jer. 31:12, 13."[15]

Things unseen can be loved because *faith* makes the invisible more vivid than the things that are seen. Thomas Manton said, "They see not Christ, because he

---

[15] Edward Reynolds, "Israel's Prayer in Time of Trouble, with God,' Gracious Answer Thereunto an Explication of the Fourteenth Chapter of Hosea," in *An Exposition of the Prophecy of Hosea*, ed. James Sherman (Edinburgh; London: James Nichol; James Nisbet & Co., 1863), 660.

is absent in Body, yet they believe in him, and love him, and send their Hearts after him."[16] It is tiresome to hear about people who say "My faith is important." Or "this fellow is a man of faith," like faith is some intangible thing they devise in their own mind, or something they see that stems from, "merely what they believe about things they like or desire." True faith is not blind, and its grounded solely on the word of God.[17]

What is it to "send the heart" after Christ? To "send the heart" after Christ is an act of faith that surpasses physical sight, anchoring the soul in the unseen yet ever-present Savior. "Whom having not seen, ye love..." (1 Peter 1:8). This sending of the heart, this love, reflects a deep spiritual yearning—a trust that fixes its gaze on Christ beyond the clouds of this world.

A believer's faith-filled love must grow in the absence of physical sight, clinging to the promise of Christ's return. This longing is not a passive hope but an active sending forth of the heart based on excited truth. Excited truth is truth that is exciting, but in the heart of the Christian, the heart is excited about it. It is a

---

[16] Thomas Manton, *A Second Volume of Sermons Preached*, (London: J. Astwood for Jonathan Robinson .., 1684), 126–127.

[17] "The godly man is a man acted by Faith... Faith cuts us off from the wild Olive of Nature, and inoculates us into Christ: Faith is the vital artery of the Soul, Hab. 2:4, "The just shall live by his Faith." Such as are destitute of Faith, though they breathe, yet they lack life; Faith is the quickener of the Graces; graces do not stir till faith sets it awork. ...Faith is a living Principle." Thomas Watson, *The Godly Mans Picture Drawn with a Scripture-Pensil*, (London: Printed for Thomas Parkhurst .., 1666), 28–29.

spiritual pursuit marked by trust, devotion, and expectation by real love.

Until the day of Christ's final return, believers are called to live by faith, rejoicing in the unseen Christ and holding fast to the certainty of His promises. Jesus foretold His glorification, saying in Matthew 26:64, "Hereafter shall ye see the Son of Man sitting on the right hand of Power, and coming in the clouds of heaven." Faith embraces this glorious truth, awaiting the fulfillment of all things.

To send the heart after Christ means fastening one's affections and desires upon Him despite His bodily absence (*holy momentum*). It is to treasure His words, cherish His promises, and live with the joyful anticipation of His return. This act of faith turns the heart heavenward, lifting it above present sorrows and distractions. Though believers cannot yet behold Christ with their physical eyes, they hold Him close through the eyes of faith. This spiritual sight is sufficient, for it sustains them until the day they see Him face to face.

In this *pursuit*, faith becomes the believer's compass, directing their heart's desire to Christ, who reigns in glory. How can one love what they do not see? They do so by true faith. How can one love what they do not know? This is impossible. The absence of sight is not a hindrance but a test of love and devotion, refining their joy and deepening their fellowship with Him. When trials obscure earthly comfort, faith steadies the soul by resting in the One who is unseen yet unfailing. To send the heart after Christ is to live as though already standing in His radiant presence, anticipating the day when faith will give way to sight and hope will be swallowed up in eternal joy.

Do you love unseen things? Is your faith increased, and does the Word help you like a conduit making the invisible more vivid than the things that are seen? There is a calling to love both God and the Lord Jesus Christ with all the heart, soul, and mind. There must be a sending of the heart out after Him.

The heart is informed by the mind. Is the mind informing the heart rightly? What is it informing? What is the substance of the information?

This love is not something that is mustered up, but a response to the divine love that was first extended. "We love Him because He first loved us," (1 John 4:19). The Gospel reveals Christ's immense love for the Church through His sacrificial death: "Christ loved the church and gave Himself for it," (Ephesians 5:25). The Holy Spirit awakens the heart to this love, pouring it in and drawing the soul into joyful devotion (Romans 5:5).

Where are such things found, but in the Scriptures? However, Scripture warns that the love of God cannot coexist with love for the world. "If any man love the world, the love of the Father is not in him," (1 John 2:15). The heart, corrupted by sin, is naturally inclined toward enmity against God (Romans 8:7). True love for God and Christ requires a reformation of the affections—a faith-rooted shift that turns desires heavenward.

This is why the Apostle Paul tells believers in Colossians 3 to *set the mind*, like concrete, on things above where Christ is. When the mind is set, the heart can be sent because it is excited by truth.

Faith and love are inseparable in this. As Paul exhorted Timothy, "Hold fast the form of sound words, which thou hast heard of me, in faith and love in Christ Jesus," (2 Timothy 1:13). Love for Christ deepens through faith, enabling a walk in confidence and joy. Peter captures this beautifully in 1 Peter 1:8: "Whom having not seen, ye love; in whom, though now ye see Him not, yet believing, ye rejoice with joy unspeakable and full of glory." Love for God produces a joy that cannot be shaken, for in Christ, the soul finds its truest delight.

This love shows itself in obedience and holiness. There is demonstration of love by worshiping God alone and revering His name (Exodus 20:3, 7). The Apostle John urges, "Little children, keep yourselves from idols," (1 John 5:21), for no other affection should occupy the heart that belongs to God. Love for God calls for holy reverence and the avoidance of anything that displeases Him. The early church, as described in Acts 9:31, was "edified and walked in the fear of the Lord." Holiness flows from this reverent love, as Paul wrote: “Perfecting holiness in the fear of God,” (2 Corinthians 7:1).

Love turns to obedience, and obedience then extends to gratitude. There is a calling to give thanks for God’s abundant blessings. Paul reminds, “In everything give thanks,” (1 Thessalonians 5:18), teaching that gratitude reflects an acknowledgment of God’s grace.

This true love for God expresses itself through trust. There is a calling to rely on God’s provision, casting all cares upon Him, knowing that He cares (1 Peter 5:7). There must be guarding against covetousness and worldly anxieties that choke out faith. Instead of striving for earthly riches, there must be finding treasure in Christ. “Godliness with contentment is great gain,” (1 Timothy 6:6).

This sending of the heart in love manifests in *diligent service*. It shows forth *holy momentum*. Paul’s charge to the Thessalonians was to “work with their own hands,” so they would lack nothing (1 Thessalonians 4:11). Love for God energizes honest labor performed with humility and reliance on His strength.

Prayer is another outflow of love. Christ Himself invites, “Ask, and it shall be given,” (Matthew 7:7). Prayer is not just a duty—it is communion with the One who is loved. Paul exhorts to “pray without ceasing,” (1 Thessalonians 5:17), for the prayer of faith sustains through every trial.

Love for God shines brightest in suffering, which is the context of Peter's exhortation. Christ warned that following Him would lead to hardship, but He also promised a reward: "Blessed are ye when men shall revile you... for great is your reward in heaven," (Matthew 5:11–12). Peter reminds, "rejoice, inasmuch as ye are partakers of Christ's sufferings," (1 Peter 4:13), for suffering refines faith and deepens fellowship with Christ. There is a calling to confess Him before others with courage, knowing that He will one day confess before the Father (Matthew 10:32).

The sending of the heart out to Christ, this love for God, must shape every word, thought, and deed. It is a living, active devotion that manifests in trust, obedience, thanksgiving, prayer, and perseverance through trials. When the heart is fixed on Christ, love endures and flourishes until the day He is seen face to face.

In all things, love for God is a living, active devotion. It informs every word, deed, and thought. True Christians love Christ not only because of what He has done but because of who He is—the altogether lovely One. Their love is marked by joyful obedience, thanksgiving, trust, prayer, and steadfastness, even amid trials. This love grows as faith deepens, sustained by the beauty of an unseen yet ever-present Savior. In this divine affection, the believer finds not only a duty fulfilled but a life transformed and a heart captivated by the Lord of Glory.

It is not such an odd thing to say or point out that things unseen can be loved greatly, even more vividly than things that are seen. It is because those things are spiritual things set down on God's revelation, the most sure Word of all things ever given.

Jonathan Edwards comments on this, "Doctrine: True religion, in great part, consists in holy affections."[18] But the importance of this is manifested when he says a few pages later: "Nothing is more manifest in Fact, than that the Things of Religion take hold of Men's Souls, no further than they affect them."[19]

Things unseen can be loved because faith makes the invisible more vivid than the things that are seen. But only to the extent that faith is excited by the Word and the Spirit. And if excited in the right way, it brings, as Peter says, an abundance of joy. "The preaching of the Word whereby faith is wrought, brings abundance of joy. That place of St. Peter is remarkable; 1 Peter 1:8. Whom having not seen, ye love; in whom, though now you see him not, yet believing, ye rejoice with joy

---

[18] Jonathan Edwards, *A Treatise Concerning Religious Affections, in Three Parts*, Early American Imprints, 1639–1800; No. 5767 (Boston: Printed for S. Kneeland and T. Green in Queen-Street, over against the prison, 1746), 3.

[19] Jonathan Edwards, *A Treatise Concerning Religious Affections, in Three Parts*, Early American Imprints, 1639–1800; No. 5767 (Boston: Printed for S. Kneeland and T. Green in Queen-Street, over against the prison, 1746), 9.

unspeakable, and full of glory: Yet believing; that is, yet exercising the acts of faith, which we too much neglect. If we did exercise these acts every day, we should have our Charter of joy renewed every day; yet believing, ye rejoice."[20]

Do you love unseen things which turn into, an abundance of joy? True faith stirs up a holy kind of wanting in the heart—a deep hunger and thirst for God and His goodness. The Bible speaks of this longing as a real sign of true faith. "With my soul have I desired thee in the night; yea, with my spirit within me will I seek thee early," (Isaiah 26:9). "One thing have I desired of the LORD, that will I seek after; that I may dwell in the house of the LORD all the days of my life, to behold the beauty of the LORD," (Psalm 27:4).

This longing is like a thirsty deer searching for water: "As the hart panteth after the water brooks, so panteth my soul after thee, O God. My soul thirsteth for God, for the living God," (Psalm 42:1–2). "O God, thou art my God; early will I seek thee: my soul thirsteth for thee, my flesh longeth for thee in a dry and thirsty land, where no water is," (Psalm 63:1).

This kind of wanting is for God Himself. It is sending the heart out after the things truly loved. "How amiable are thy tabernacles, O LORD of hosts! My soul

---

[20] James Ussher, *Twenty Sermons Preached at Oxford before His Majesty, and Elsewhere*, (London: Printed for Nathanael Ranew .., 1678), 152.

longeth, yea, even fainteth for the courts of the LORD," (Psalm 84:1–2).

Jesus Himself called this hunger a blessing: "Blessed are they which do hunger and thirst after righteousness: for they shall be filled," (Matthew 5:6). When there is longing for God and His goodness, there is the promise of satisfaction from Him.

Sometimes *not seeing* is difficult. But seeing through the eyes of the Word is set in *joy unspeakable* and it fuels *holy momentum*. To trust God on His bare Word is to love Him without needing to see Him with the eyes. This is exactly what Peter teaches: "Though now ye see him not, yet believing, ye rejoice with joy unspeakable and full of glory," (1 Peter 1:8).

Faith is built not on physical sight of Christ but on the beauty of Christ revealed through His Word. The world asks how anyone can love someone never seen. But the answer stands: love is grounded in who Christ is as revealed in Scripture.

Faith is the bridge between what is unseen and what is true. "Esteeming the reproach of Christ greater riches than the treasures in Egypt: for he had respect unto the recompence of the reward... for he endured, as seeing him who is invisible," (Hebrews 11:26–27). The treasures of the world fade, but the truth of Christ's love does not change.

This kind of love causes the world to pause. When there is trusting in nothing but God's Word, it confounds them. It shows that God is trustworthy because of who He is, not because of what is seen. The early Christians endured suffering with joy because they trusted the unseen Christ and His promise of eternal glory.

Peter reminds that loving the unseen Christ brings "joy unspeakable and full of glory" (1 Peter 1:8). That joy itself becomes a testimony. When there is enduring trials with hope, giving up earthly gain for eternal treasure, and worshiping through hardship, faith is displayed in action.

Loving Christ based on His Word strengthens the believer. "I will never leave thee, nor forsake thee," (Hebrews 13:5). "In the world ye shall have tribulation: but be of good cheer; I have overcome the world," (John 16:33). Trusting His Word means believing that His promises outweigh every earthly offer.

It is saying that loss for Christ is never loss in Christ. When the heart is sent after Him in this way, the world takes notice. Faith becomes a declaration that His Word is enough because He is enough. And when the final day comes, unseen faith will become sight, and the One trusted will welcome His people into everlasting joy.

Things unseen can be loved because faith makes the invisible more vivid than the things that are seen.

Conclusion: The Full Course of Holy Momentum

Holy Momentum is the God-fashioned movement of the believer from beginning to end—rooted in covenant promise, exercised in present dependence, directed toward eternal glory, marked by separation from the world, and sustained by love for the unseen Christ. What has been unfolded across these chapters is not a collection of disconnected doctrines, but one continuous current of divine action in the life of God's people. It begins before a man is aware of it, carries him through every season of life, and extends beyond him into generations yet unborn, until it finds its final rest in the appearing of Christ. Let's consider it all in conclusion.

Chapter 1: The Righteous Man and His Seed After Him

Holy Momentum does not begin with man—it begins with *God's covenant*. The righteous man stands not as an isolated individual, but as one situated within the purposes of God that extend beyond his own lifetime. Scripture establishes this plainly: "His seed shall be mighty upon earth: the generation of the upright shall be blessed," (Psalm 112:2). The life of the righteous man is not self-contained; it is generationally influential. God orders His dealings so that the faith, obedience, and dependence of one life become, the means by which others are brought into the same current of grace.

This is seen in the patriarchs. Abraham walked by promise. Isaac inherited that promise. Jacob clung to it in weakness. The God of Abraham, Isaac, and Jacob is not merely identified by names—He is identified by continuity. Holy Momentum moves from father to son, from one generation to the next, not by human power, but by divine faithfulness.

In this way, the righteous man does not simply live—he *establishes* a *trajectory*. His calling upon God, his leaning upon Christ, his obedience in trial, his ordering of his household—these form a pattern. His seed sees it, hears it, and is shaped by it. Holy Momentum, therefore, is not only personal movement—it is *covenantal* movement. It carries forward through lineage, through teaching, through example, until God gathers His people across all generations into one inheritance.

Chapter 2: Call Upon Me in Trouble

Yet this momentum is not sustained by heritage alone. It is renewed continually in dependence. The believer must learn what Jacob learned, what David learned, what every saint must learn: movement with God is maintained by calling upon Him. "Call upon me in the day of trouble: I will deliver thee, and thou shalt glorify me," (Psalm 50:15).

This is not merely instruction—it is *structure*. Trouble is certain. Calling is commanded. Deliverance is promised. Glory is required. Holy Momentum is carried forward through this repeated cycle. The believer is pressed by trouble, lifted by prayer, delivered by God, and returned to praise. This is the pulse of the Christian life.

Without calling upon God, momentum *halts*. The soul begins to rely on itself, to reason apart from Scripture, to seek help from the world. But when the believer calls upon God rightly—in faith, humility, fervency, and submission—God answers. Not always by removing the trial, but always by sustaining the soul. Thus, Holy Momentum is not the absence of trouble—it is the advancement through trouble by divine help.

Chapter 3: The Day of the Lord

This movement is not without direction. It is aimed toward a fixed and certain end—the Day of the Lord. "But the day of the Lord will come as a thief in the night," (2 Peter 3:10). The believer moves forward with this day in view. It is the day of final judgment, of cosmic dissolution, of perfect justice, and of eternal separation between the righteous and the wicked.

This day gives weight to every step. "Seeing then that all these things shall be dissolved, what manner of persons ought ye to be in all holy conversation and godliness," (2 Peter 3:11). Holy Momentum is not aimless motion—it is purposeful progression toward accountability before Christ.

The Day of the Lord carries a dual edge. It is terror for the wicked and triumph for the righteous. It is the day when Christ will appear in glory, "and every eye shall see him," (Revelation 1:7). It is the day when the faithful will be vindicated and the ungodly judged. This certainty presses urgency into the present life. The believer does not drift—he prepares. He does not delay—he pursues holiness.

In this way, *Holy Momentum* is shaped by eternity. Every act, every prayer, every trial, every step is taken, in light of that coming day.

Chapter 4: Leave the World Behind

But movement toward God requires separation from the world. Jacob's testimony captures this plainly: "For with my staff I passed over this Jordan; and now I am become two bands," (Genesis 32:10). He left with nothing but a staff and a promise. The world behind him offered no security. His future offered no visible certainty. But God had spoken.

To leave the world behind is not to despise God's creation, but to reject false reliance upon it. The believer must loosen his grip on earthly comforts, riches, honors, and pleasures. These things, though lawful in measure, become snares when they compete with God. Holy Momentum requires lightness of soul—freedom from entanglement.

The staff becomes the emblem of this life. It represents weakness upheld, frailty supported, and dependence embodied. Jacob did not stand by strength—he leaned. And this leaning is not a sign of infirmity, but of wisdom. "Thy rod and thy staff they comfort me," (Psalm 23:4). The believer moves forward by leaning on God's promises, not by trusting his own ability.

In this way, *Holy Momentum* is marked by surrender. The believer walks forward, not loaded with worldly securities, but sustained by divine faithfulness. He leaves the world behind because he has found something greater.

Chapter 5: Loving Things Unseen

At the heart of this movement lies a weighty reality: the believer is drawn forward by love for an unseen Christ. "Whom having not seen, ye love; in whom, though now ye see him not, yet believing, ye rejoice with joy unspeakable and full of glory," (1 Peter 1:8).

This is the *inward engine* of Holy Momentum. Faith makes the invisible more vivid than the visible. The believer does not move merely by duty or fear, but by affection. Christ, though unseen, becomes the most real and most desirable object of the soul.

This love produces joy—"joy unspeakable and full of glory." It produces obedience—"If ye love me, keep my commandments," (John 14:15). It produces perseverance—enduring trials with hope and confidence. The believer's heart is sent out after Christ, longing for Him, trusting Him, delighting in Him.

In this way, Holy Momentum is not forced—it is drawn. The believer moves forward because he loves Christ. He presses on because Christ is precious. He endures because Christ is worth it.

The Whole Course

When these chapters are taken together, the full course of Holy Momentum is seen. It begins with God establishing a righteous man whose life extends into his seed. It continues as that man calls upon God in the day of trouble and learns dependence. It is directed by the certainty of the Day of the Lord, giving purpose and urgency. It is marked by leaving the world behind and walking with nothing but God's promise. It is sustained and energized by love for the unseen Christ. And it ends in glory.

The believer who began with nothing but a staff will stand before Christ with everything fulfilled. The one who called upon God will hear Him answer fully. The one who lived, in light of that day will stand ready in it. The one who left the world behind will inherit a better world. The one who loved the unseen Christ will see Him face to face. This is *Holy Momentum.*

It is not man climbing to God—it is God carrying man. It is not strength—it is grace. It is not sight—it is faith. It is not stagnation—it is movement. And it continues—through prayer, through trial, through generations—until that final and greatest day, when faith becomes sight, and the movement of grace gives way to everlasting rest in the presence of the Lord Jesus Christ.

Other Works by Dr. McMahon at Puritan Publications

5 Marks of a Biblical Church

5 Marks of a Biblical Disciple

5 Marks of Biblical Commitment to the Visible Body of Christ

5 Marks of Biblical Reformation

5 Marks of Christian Resolve

5 Marks of Devotion to God

A Heart for Reformation

A Primer on the Art of Expository Preaching

A Practical Guide to Primeval History

A Simple Overview of Covenant Theology

A Watchman Over Christ's Church

Augustine's Calvinism: The Doctrines of Grace in Augustine's Writings

Bah Humbug: How Christians Should Think About the Christmas Holiday

Being with Jesus

Christ Commanding His Coronavirus to Covenant Breakers

Christ the Apple Tree and the Joy of True Religion

Covenant Theology Made Easy

Eternity Weighed in the Balance

Following Christ Whithersoever He Goes

Gradual Reformation Intolerable

Historical Theology Made Easy

How Faith Works: Rescuing the Gospel from Contemporary Evangelicalism

How to Live Every Day in the End Times

I Am for You: God's Power in Supporting His People

John 3:16

John Calvin's View of God's Love and the Doctrine of Reprobation

Joseph's Resolve and the Unreasonableness of Sinning Against God

Overcoming Lust In a Sex-crazed World

Practical Observations on the Book of Jude

Practical Observations on the Book of Ruth

Practical Observations on the Lord's Prayer

Practical Observations on the Lord's Supper

Psalm 96: A Theology of Praise 2nd Edition

Reformation of the Heart, Soul and Mind

Save Me: A Study of Psalm 119:89-96

Seeing Christ Clearly

Sophia and the Umbrella – A Children's Book on Justification

Sparks of Divine Glory: A Practical Study of the Attributes of God

Systematic Theology Made Easy

The Cage: A Young Children's Guide to the Biblical Teaching on Hell

The Five Principles of the Gospel

The Kingdom of Heaven is Upon You

The Lord's Voice Cries to the City: A Biblical Guide for Hearing the Word of God Preached

The Reformation Made Easy

The Reformed Apprentice: A Workbook on Reformed Theology (Volumes 1-4)

The Ten Commandments in the Life of the Christian

The Two Wills of God Made Easy

The Two Wills of God: Does God Really Have Two Wills?

The Wickedness, Humiliation, Restoration and Reformation of Manasseh

Umiko and the Mask – Children's Book on Election

Underneath the Blood

Unmasking Self-Flattery in the Church

Walking Victoriously in the Power of the Spirit

www.ingramcontent.com/pod-product-compliance
Lightning Source LLC
LaVergne TN
LVHW051002080826
845145LV00009B/2413

* 9 7 8 1 6 2 6 6 3 5 4 7 0 *